DIRECT DEMOCRACY AND MINORITY RIGHTS

This book conclusively demonstrates that direct democracy—institutions like the ballot initiative and the referendum—endangers the rights of minorities and perpetuates a tyranny of the majority. While advocates of direct democracy claim that these institutions protect citizens from corrupt lawmakers beholden to special interests, Daniel Lewis' thorough investigation shows how such mass participation exposes minority groups to negative policy outcomes favored by only a slim majority of voters.

While research has been presented that supports both sides of the debate, the existing literature has yet to produce consistent and compelling evidence in favor of one side or the other. This book undertakes a comprehensive examination of the "tyranny of the majority" critique of direct democracy by examining a host of contemporary American state policies that affect the rights of a variety of minority groups. By assessing the impact of direct democracy on both ballot measures and traditional legislation, the book provides a more complete picture of how citizen legislative institutions can affect minority rights, covering a myriad of contemporary minority rights issues, including same-sex marriage, affirmative action, racial profiling, and anti-discrimination laws.

The book is unique in its approach and scope, making it compelling for scholars interested in direct democracy, state politics, minority politics, and electoral institutions, as well as American politics generally.

Daniel C. Lewis is an Assistant Professor of Political Science at the University of New Orleans. His research examines state political institutions and public policy. His work on direct democracy, legislative term limits, policy diffusion, LGBT politics, and federalism has been published in a number of leading political science journals.

Controversies in Electoral Democracy and Representation
Matthew J. Streb, Series Editor

The Routledge series *Controversies in Electoral Democracy and Representation* presents cutting-edge scholarship and innovative thinking on a broad range of issues relating to democratic practice and theory. An electoral democracy, to be effective, must show a strong relationship between representation and a fair, open election process. Designed to foster debate and challenge assumptions about how elections and democratic representation *should* work, titles in the series present a strong but fair argument on topics related to elections, voting behavior, party and media involvement, representation, and democratic theory.

Titles in the series:

DIRECT DEMOCRACY AND MINORITY RIGHTS

A Critical Assessment of the Tyranny of the Majority in the American States

Daniel C. Lewis

Routledge
Taylor & Francis Group

NEW YORK AND LONDON

First published 2013
by Routledge
711 Third Avenue, New York, NY 10017

Simultaneously published in the UK
by Routledge
2 Park Square, Milton Park, Abingdon, Oxon OX14 4RN

Routledge is an imprint of the Taylor & Francis Group, an informa business

© 2013 Taylor & Francis

Library of Congress Cataloging in Publication Data
Lewis, Daniel C.
   Direct democracy and minority rights: a critical assessment of the tyranny of the majority in the American states/Daniel C. Lewis.
   p. cm.—(Controversies in electoral democracy and representation)
   Includes bibliographical references and index.
   1. Direct democracy—United States—States.   2. Representative government and representation—United States—States.   3. Majorities.
   4. Minorities—Civil rights—United States—States.   I. Title.
   JF494.L48 2012
   323.173—dc23
   2012018205

ISBN: 978–0–415–53743–8 (hbk)
ISBN: 978–0–415–53744–5 (pbk)
ISBN: 978–0–203–10934–2 (ebk)

Typeset in Bembo and Stone Sans
by Florence Production Ltd, Stoodleigh, Devon, UK

SUSTAINABLE FORESTRY INITIATIVE
Certified Sourcing
www.sfiprogram.org
SFI-00555
The SFI label applies to the text stock.

Printed and bound in the United States of America by Walsworth Publishing Company, Marceline, MO.

To Chief and Her Majesty
. . . a real writer and his muse.

CONTENTS

FIGURES

TABLES

ACKNOWLEDGMENTS

This book is the result of over seven years of study on the topic of direct democracy and minority rights. Over this time period, I have received invaluable personal and professional support from numerous individuals. The project began at Michigan State University under the able tutelage of Saundra Schneider. I could not have completed the project without her support and guidance. I also owe many thanks to William Jacoby, Richard Hula, Elisabeth Gerber, Belinda Davis, and Frederick Wood.

Portions of this book have been presented at a variety of professional conferences, where I have been very fortunate to get helpful feedback from my fellow state politics scholars. In particular, I owe a debt of gratitude to Daniel Smith, Justin Phillips, Joshua Dyck, Todd Donovan, and Thomas Carsey for their helpful comments and suggestions. I'd also like to thank the organizers and participants of the annual State Politics and Policy conference (especially Christopher Z. Mooney), which has been a critical resource for my academic development.

In the past four years, I've worked at the Department of Political Science at the University of New Orleans. For their helpful advice in further advancing the project, I'd like to thank Christine Day, Matthew Jacobsmeier, Richard Frank, and Elizabeth Stein. I'd also like to thank Michael Huelshoff, Robert Montjoy, Salmon Shomade, Edward Chervenak, and Denise Strong for their support and collegiality.

Earlier versions of the analyses of same-sex marriage bans appeared in, "Direct Democracy and Minority Rights: Same-Sex Marriage Bans in the U.S. States," published in *Social Science Quarterly* (2011). A form of Chapter 3 was published in *State Politics and Policy Quarterly* (2011) as "Bypassing the Representational Filter? Minority Rights Policies under Direct Democracy Institutions in the U.S. States." I thank editors Robert Lineberry, Ronald Keith Gaddie, Kelly Damphousse, Thad

Kousser, Ronald Weber, Richard Winters, and the anonymous reviewers for their help in developing these sections of the book.

I also need to thank the team at Routledge, including my editor, Michael Kerns, and editorial assistant, Darcy Bullock. I am very grateful for the support and patience of Michael, who worked with me to move the project from a proposal to a full manuscript. I also thank Matthew Streb for his encouragement in pursuing this project as part of the *Controversies in Electoral Democracy and Representation* series.

Finally, I thank my amazingly supportive family—Liz, Bridger, and Delilah— who have given me a critical counterbalance to the pressures of pursuing a doctoral degree and launching an academic career. They have been patient, supportive, and loving throughout. I am truly blessed.

1

DIRECT DEMOCRACY INSTITUTIONS AND THE THREAT OF TYRANNY

On November 7, 2006 Michigan voters cast ballots to ban affirmative action programs in the state. That same day, citizens of Colorado voted to amend their constitution to prohibit recognition of same-sex marriages and Arizona voters passed a constitutional amendment to require virtually all government actions to be conducted in English. Each of these policies restricts the rights of minority groups based on their race, ethnicity, gender, sexual orientation, or national origin. Each policy was enacted through citizen legislation rather than through the traditional legislative process. Unfortunately for minority groups in the United States, these three states were not alone in passing policies that restrict minority rights through direct democracy processes like ballot initiatives and referenda. In all, twelve ballot measures in ten states addressed the rights of minority groups in 2006. Eleven of these measures resulted in an anti-minority outcome. These policy enactments and other similar outcomes resulting from citizen legislation in recent years have raised concerns about the security of the rights of minority groups in states with direct democracy institutions. This book examines this matter through a series of analyses of contemporary policies that directly affect minority groups.

So, does direct democracy endanger minority rights? Despite the recent attention to this question, it is not a new concern. Rather, this issue has long been at the center of the debate over whether states should allow citizens to create public policy directly through institutions like the ballot initiative and popular referendum. Advocates of direct democracy institutions argue that citizen legislation protects the public by allowing it to circumvent corrupt lawmakers that are beholden to special interests.[1] Though supporters of direct democracy reforms concede that anti-minority outcomes are possible with citizen legislation, they contend that these outcomes are no more prevalent than under traditional representative policymaking institutions.[2] The counter-argument asserts that mass participation exposes minority groups to potentially tyrannical policy outcomes favored by only a slim majority of the voters (i.e., 50 percent plus one). Minority rights are put at heightened risk under direct democracy institutions because they allow the majority to circumvent the checks and balances of a representative, separated powers system that is designed to encourage deliberation and minority representation.

Unfortunately, the existing scholarly literature does not give a clear indication as to which side of the debate is supported empirically. Studies have been published that show support for both sides of the debate, but they are limited in their scope and their ability to draw conclusions that apply broadly across different issue areas and political systems.[3] In his recent examination of direct democracy and policy congruence, John G. Matsusaka, president of the Initiative and Referendum Institute and a leading direct democracy scholar, succinctly summarizes the unsettled nature of the debate over direct democracy and minority rights:

> In short, we simply do not have compelling evidence yet on whether initiatives or legislatures pose a greater threat to minority rights, or even if there is a difference. The most defensible position is one of agnosticism: pending more evidence, we just don't know.[4]

This book seeks to address this "agnosticism" in the debate surrounding the impact of direct democracy on minority rights by taking a more systematic examination of contemporary policies that affect the rights of a variety of minority groups across the United States. This study expands beyond the previous literature by accounting for both the direct and indirect impacts of direct democracy on minority rights through examinations of policy outcomes from both citizen legislation and traditional legislation. It also expands upon the previous literature by directly comparing policy decisions in direct democracy states to decisions in non-direct democracy states while examining both anti-minority policies as well as pro-minority policies. In doing so, the empirical evidence reveals a clear majoritarian effect of direct democracy. In other words, the ability of citizens to directly create public policy increases governmental responsiveness to the preferences of the majority. In cases where the majority prefers policies that restrict the rights of political minorities, this enhanced responsiveness works to the detriment of these groups.

Direct Democracy in the American States

Before exploring the effects that direct democracy may have on minority rights, it is helpful to consider how direct democracy became such a prevalent form of policymaking in the United States. From its founding, American government was designed as a representative democracy. A central tenet for architects of the newly independent nation and its states was that the authority and legitimacy to govern derived from the consent of the citizens. At the same time, these revolutionaries were also concerned with protecting against various forms of tyranny stemming from the ills of factions.[5] In designing a representative democratic system of government they were able to link the public, from which the government's authority was derived, to policymakers through regular elections, and thus make elected officials sensitive to public preferences. Any further direct participation by the public was viewed as unwise and even dangerous to the fledgling republic.

Apart from the ratification of constitutional amendments and state constitutions, the first century of governance in the United States was executed solely through representative democracy. By the end of the nineteenth century, however, dissatisfaction with government policies on a range of issues began to sow the seeds of a populist movement to increase public participation in government.[6] In an era of rapid industrialization, corporate monopolies, and boom-and-bust cycles in both farming and mining, farmers, laborers, miners and other "plain folk" advocated for policies such as free silver coinage, graduated income taxes, public ownership of railroads, and single taxes. All of these policies sought to wrest economic power away from moneyed special interests, like trusts and corporations. Unfortunately for populist forces, both the national parties and the legislatures were often controlled by these economic behemoths. Party bosses and machine politics controlled much of the legislative process, especially at the local and state levels. In order to achieve their varied economic reforms, populists soon realized they would first have to pursue political reform.

Populist theories of governance assert that government policy should reflect the "will of the people." Furthermore, this public "will" or preference can be identified through a public vote.[7] In short, populists equated the will of the people with the majority position of the voting public. Most farmers, laborers and single-taxers believed that their positions were supported by the majority of the people, and construed government inaction on their issues as a sign of how government had been captured by special interests. With the public will effectively subverted by representative government, the Populist movement (and later Progressives) sought to increase public participation in government as a way to force government to reflect the public will. The direct democracy tools of initiatives, referenda, and recall elections gained prominence in the Populist platform following the publication of J. W. Sullivan's *Direct Legislation by the Citizenship through the Initiative and Referendum* in 1893. Sullivan had traveled to Switzerland and became enamored with their system of direct democracy that was modeled on the ancient tradition of *Landsgemeinde*, annual open-air meetings where all men of the canton would decide the policies of the local government.[8] In addition to Sullivan's writings, other advocates of direct democracy also touted initiatives and referenda as institutions to circumvent unresponsive legislatures. Nathan Cree claimed that direct democracy would "break the crushing and stifling power of our great party machines."[9]

Direct democracy reforms were soon viewed as the most viable means to achieve varied economic policy goals of populist groups. By the end of the nineteenth century, direct democracy was also viewed as way to implement social policy. Women's suffrage groups and prohibitionists soon took up advocacy of initiatives and referenda. What had once been a working-class issue had now achieved more broad-based support as more and more groups saw direct democracy as an acceptable means to pursue their own policy goals. Despite the egalitarian rhetoric of the initiative and referendum movement, support for these reforms was also undeniably influenced by self-interest and more narrow policy preferences.[10]

Nonetheless, the Populist and Progressive movements for "good government" through direct democracy spread throughout the country at the turn of the century, especially in the West and Midwest. Though direct democracy institutions force legislatures to cede policymaking power to citizens, the growing popularity of these reforms created electoral incentives for legislators to support them. Smith and Fridkin find that legislatures in states with the most competitive electoral climate were more likely to pass direct democracy reforms as the two parties fought for control of state government.[11] In these states, legislators were willing to relinquish some institutional power in exchange for electoral gains and partisan power.

The 1890s saw the first adoptions of ballot initiatives in cities and states. South Dakota became the first state to adopt initiatives and referenda in 1898. Over the next twenty years, eighteen more states followed (see Figure 1.1). The adoptions of direct legislation institutions then ceased until 1959, when Alaska became a state. Following Alaska, four more states and the District of Columbia have also adopted some form of the initiative. As of 2000, these twenty-four states (and the District of Columbia) comprised almost half of the population of the United States. At the local level, Matsusaka shows that fifteen of the twenty most populous cities in the country have ballot initiatives.[12]

Though almost half of the American states allow for direct citizen participation in the policy process through some form of citizen legislation, the arrangements of these institutions vary considerably across the states. There are three basic types of citizen legislation: direct initiatives, indirect initiatives, and popular referenda. Direct initiatives are the most analogous to pure democracy: They completely bypass the legislature. Under this institutional arrangement citizens can draft policy proposals, petition to place them on the ballot, and then vote to accept or reject the policy. Indirect initiatives are similar, except that they must be submitted to the legislature for consideration before they are placed on the ballot. This arrangement allows the legislature to craft an alternative measure and place it on the ballot alongside the citizens' proposal. Popular referenda, meanwhile, do not originate with the citizens. Rather, citizens can gather signatures to place an enacted piece of legislation on the ballot for the people to reject or accept.

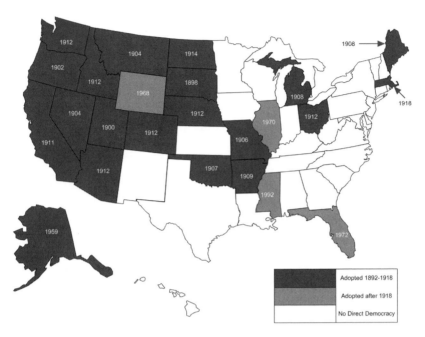

FIGURE 1.1 State Adoptions of Direct Democracy Institutions

In addition to these three basic types of citizen legislation, states also vary in the rules and regulations that concern their direct democracy provisions (see Table 1.1). Some states allow citizen legislation for both statutes and constitutional amendments. Others can only use these mechanisms for one or the other. In terms of content, most states have a single-subject rule that limits logrolling phenomena that could occur through the bundling of multiple policies on a single ballot measure. This restriction avoids problems associated with omnibus bills where none of the various components of a bill has majority support, but bundled together can garner enough support to pass. It also addresses the issues of unrelated policy riders that are tacked on to popular measures and pass despite having little support in the electorate. Many states also have further content restrictions. For example, Alaska does not allow ballot measures that concern appropriations or revenues. In Nebraska, the same subject cannot appear on the ballot more than once in three years. Wyoming does not allow ballot measures concerning the judiciary.

Another area of variation is in the petition requirements. Massachusetts only requires the signatures of 3.5 percent of the electorate from the preceding gubernatorial election, while Maine requires 10 percent. Most states base their signature requirements on votes cast in the most recent gubernatorial election, which usually has high turnout, but others use the previous general election, whose

TABLE 1.1 Direct Legislation Institutions

State	Type	Single subject	Content restrictions	Signature requirements	
				Statutory	Constitutional
Alaska	I, R	▲	▲	10★	—
Arizona	D, R	▲		10	15
Arkansas	D, R			8★	10★
California	D, R	▲		5	8
Colorado	D, R	▲		5	5
Florida	D	▲		—	8★
Idaho	D, R	▲		10★	—
Illinois	D	▲		—	8
Maine	I, R			10	—
Massachusetts	I, R	▲	▲	3 + 0.5★ᵃ	3★
Michigan	D, I, R	▲		8	10
Mississippi	I		▲	—	12★
Missouri	D, R	▲	▲	5★	8★
Montana	D, R	▲	▲	5★	10★
Nebraska	D, R	▲	▲	7★	10★
Nevada	D, I, R	▲	▲	10★	10★
North Dakota	D, R	▲	▲	2ᵇ	4ᵇ
Ohio	D, I, R	▲	▲	3 + 3★ᵃ	10★
Oklahoma	D, R	▲		8	15
Oregon	D, R	▲		6	8
South Dakota	D, R	▲		6	8
Utah	D, I, R	▲		5 + 5★ᵃ	—
Washington	D, I, R	▲		8	—
Wyoming	I, R	▲	▲	15★	—

Notes:

D indicates direct initiatives, I indicates indirect initiatives, R indicates popular referenda; Signature requirements are a percentage of a previous election unless otherwise indicated. ★Indicates a geographic distribution requirement.

a The first figure is the percent needed for a proposal to be referred to the legislature and the second figure is the additional percent needed to place the measure on the ballot if the legislature does not pass it.
b North Dakota's signature requirement is a percentage of the resident population.

turnout can vary depending on the races at the top of the ballot. North Dakota's signature requirements, meanwhile, are based on the resident population. Signature requirements can be further complicated with geographic distribution rules. For example, Alaska requires at least one signature from two-thirds of the electoral districts in the state.

These variations in the institutional arrangements are not trivial. They create minimum thresholds of support that can deter or encourage citizen lawmaking. The difficulty in placing a policy proposal on the ballot can affect how much citizen legislation is used in a state, and thus can affect its impact on public policy.[13] The institutional arrangements of direct democracy can also have an impact on the power of the legislature to influence policy relative to its citizens. Bowler and Donovan have shown that both qualification difficulty and the insulation of the legislature in direct democracy states have significant effects on policy outcomes.[14]

The Impact of Direct Democracy

Undoubtedly, the adoption of direct democracy reforms has added new features to the policy process in many of the American states. By allowing direct citizen participation in the state-level policy process, the direct democracy reforms of the past century have most certainly also altered the policy outcomes in these states. This influence on state policy outcomes has important consequences for public policy in the United States. State governments have long had significant authority over critical policy areas, such as education and elections. In addition, scholars have noted the resurgence of the American states in policy prominence and institutional capacity in the past few decades.[15] Recent trends in federal policy, like the devolution of programmatic responsibility of Medicaid and welfare to the states, have further increased the significance of state-level policy in the lives of American citizens. The upshot of all of this is that direct democracy reforms have influenced important policy outcomes across the American states. The question that follows is: How exactly have these policies been affected?

It's true that populist and progressive groups pursued direct democracy reforms like the initiative and referendum as a means to enact their specific policy goals, but they also saw these institutions as a way to make policy *in general* more reflective of the public will. While several states used direct democracy to pass progressive reforms like the prohibition of liquor sales and women's suffrage, other policy areas, from taxes to abortion, have also been addressed through ballot initiatives and referenda. Since 1980, governmental reforms, like term limits and campaign finance laws, and tax policies have been the most common issues addressed by ballot initiatives. Social and moral policies, as well as environmental policies, have also been common subjects of recent ballot initiatives.[16] So while direct democracy reforms have certainly served the specific policy goals of the progressive and populist movements, the adoption of citizen legislative institutions have also had a broader effect on virtually all state policy areas.

Still, it is not clear that these reforms have brought policy outcomes closer to the public will. If it is assumed that the policy preferences of the majority do accurately reflect the general will of the public, then these reforms may be considered successful. Indeed, empirical studies have found that, for many policy areas, outcomes in direct democracy states are more reflective of the majority preference than in non-direct democracy states.[17] Matsusaka shows that, in general, initiatives do produce policies favored by the majority of the population.[18]

By circumventing the legislature, initiatives allow citizens to pass policies favored by the majority without obstruction from the legislature or special interests. In addition, recent studies have shown that initiatives can have an indirect effect on polices enacted by the legislature.[19] With the threat of citizen legislation, policies passed by the legislature in direct democracy states tend to be more congruent with the preferences of the majority.

Although contemporary academic studies have supported the claims of the early direct democracy advocates in terms of increased governmental responsiveness to the majority, most of this research does not provide guidance on the normative nature of these effects. Is this type of responsiveness beneficial to American democracy? Are there negative consequences to these reforms? Critics of direct democracy institutions have long contended that a government that is hyper-responsive to the public may be worse than a government that is less responsive. From this perspective, the mass public is considered to be a relatively ignorant, irresponsible, and capricious group.[20] Responsiveness to the masses would only produce rash and unwise policies. Another problem that opponents of direct democracy identify is the assumption that the public will (as defined and identified by populists) equates to the public interest. If the public will is simply the preference of the majority of the public, then minority interests and preferences will be routinely overlooked, and even intentionally targeted. By making government responsive only to the preferences of the majority, minority rights could be put at risk.

Direct Democracy and Minority Rights: Tyranny of the Majority?

Concern about the rights of minorities in democratic societies extends far beyond the direct democracy debate sparked by the Populist and Progressive movements of the twentieth century. In designing America's democratic institutions, the framers of the Constitution frequently cited the protection of minority rights as justification for their form of representative government. James Madison noted the importance of guarding "one part of the society against the injustice of the other part," and warned that, "If a majority be united by a common interest, the rights of the minority will be insecure."[21] He further argues that pure democracy, in which citizens participate directly, cannot cope with the ills of factions because there is no check on the power of the majority to rule at the expense of minorities. With these concerns in mind, Madison vigorously opposed many forms of direct citizen participation, from citizen legislation to the direct election of senators and the president, and offered representative government as an alternative governmental design that would better protect minority rights.

Thus, the mischief of factions was to be thwarted by the filtering processes of representative democratic government. The Federalists argued that raw public opinion could be "refine[d] and enlarge[d] . . . by passing through a medium of a chosen body of citizens."[22] This representational filter is designed to work by emphasizing deliberation, compromise, and consensus-building. Although the agenda-setting power of contemporary American political parties may mitigate some of these filtering mechanisms to a small extent, the legislative process nonetheless continues to stress deliberation, compromise, and consensus-building in its design.[23]

Obviously, legislatures allow minority groups to obtain some degree of representation in the policy process, as well as a voice in policy debates via their elected representatives. In addition, the process itself can create a bargaining environment conducive to cooperation and moderation. Bills face a daunting gauntlet of obstacles on their way to passage. At each point, from committee mark-ups to bicameral conference reports, legislation can be changed and refined in order to build the necessary consensus for enactment. In general, a fairly large coalition of support is essential to pass anything through this process. Building a large legislative coalition provides incentives to compromise in order to attract the requisite support for passage. Thus, the traditional legislative process allows for ample consideration of interests on both sides of an issue, which should help to ensure minority representation, and also provides incentives for legislators to compromise and produce more moderate policy.[24]

In addition to allowing for minority representation through the electoral connection, representative democracy also provides organized minority groups multiple access points from which to promote their interests in a way that citizen legislation does not allow. This is not to say that organized interests do not play a significant role in policymaking under direct democracy institutions. Studies have shown that interest groups may actually benefit from these institutions.[25] Rather, reducing meaningful access by political minorities to the policy process can limit the advancement of their interests. Furthermore, the dominance of citizen groups that mobilize around moral and social issues in direct democracy processes can actually exacerbate the problem of protecting minority rights.[26]

Another aspect of the representational filter is that the legislative process places a premium on relationship-building. Legislative decision-making is not a one-shot game. Instead, legislators work with each other again and again across a myriad of issues and policies. It would be ill-advised for legislators to completely shut out their minority colleagues on one issue since they may be needed for consensus on another issue. Thus, the legislative process, itself, provides both opportunity and incentives for the kind of deliberation and compromise that should help protect minority rights. In circumventing this representational legislative process, direct democracy affords little opportunity for minority voices to be heard and creates more rigid legislation that requires far less consensus, especially from interested minority groups.[27]

Direct democracy also provides opponents of minority rights a relatively easy way to achieve their goals by quickly expanding the scope of conflict from the legislative arena to the public forum.[28] Compared with a ballot measure, where millions of citizens may participate, the relatively small arena of a state legislature allows minority voices to be part of the deliberation and debate. As such, minority groups can often contribute to the policy debate through the filtering processes of representative government. However, in expanding the scope of conflict to the mass level, majoritarian preferences can easily overwhelm any consideration of minority rights.

Figures 1.2a and 1.2b illustrate the majoritarian effect of direct democracy through very stylized diagrams of the legislative process. Figure 1.2a shows the policy process in a state with a traditional, representative democratic system. Public preferences (among other inputs), conceptualized here broadly as the opinions of the entire public, are filtered through representative democratic institutions. The filtering mechanisms of deliberation, representation, and coalition-building all help protect the rights of minorities, albeit imperfectly. Thus, the representative system generates policy decisions that are products of all public preferences and the filtering mechanisms.

Figure 1.2b, meanwhile, shows the policy process in a state with direct democracy institutions. Under this system there are two paths to reach policy decisions. First, the representative democratic institutions can set policy through a process similar to the one shown in Figure 1.2a. Second, citizens can circumvent the legislature and its filtering mechanism and create policy directly. In the second path, the policy outcome is wholly dependent on the preferences of the majority of the electorate since policy decisions on this path are determined by a plurality vote. This second path is the *direct* impact of direct democracy on policy decisions where majority preferences are transferred directly into policy decisions.

FIGURE 1.2A Policy Process under a Representative Democratic System

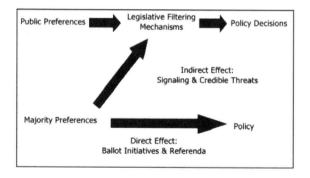

FIGURE 1.2B Policy Process under a System with Direct Democracy Institutions

In addition to the *direct* impact ballot initiatives and referenda can have on policy decisions, their potential use by the public also has *indirect* effects (as shown by the arrow connecting majority preferences to the legislative filters). This indirect impact works by altering the expectations that legislators have about the policy process and subsequently altering their strategic decision-making.[29] The influence of direct democracy institutions is felt by legislators in two ways: It can send clear signals about the policy preferences of the majority and it can serve as a credible threat to enact a particular policy. By sending clear signals as to the preferences of the majority, legislators will be pressured to adopt policies closer to these preferences. As an alternative policymaking path, citizen legislation allows the majority to credibly threaten to enact extreme policies. Legislators may respond to this threat by preempting the citizen legislation and passing a more moderate version of the policy. Either way, the use or threatened use of ballot initiatives and referenda forces legislators to be more cognizant and responsive to the majority. Legislators may also move to preempt citizen legislation in order to claim credit for popular policies as well as to mitigate more extreme policy decisions.

In altering the behavior of legislators to make them more responsive to majority preferences, this indirect effect of direct democracy also reduces the access that organized minority groups might otherwise have in the traditional legislative process. Legislators that are induced to be responsive to majority preferences through the threat of citizen legislation may not be less willing to listen to groups that represent of minority interests. Thus, the indirect impact may serve to undermine the influence of all types of organized interests in the legislative process, including minority interests. Further, this deflation of lobbying power should also extend to the executive agencies that implement policy passed by the legislature. Work by Kenneth Meier shows that bureaucracies can serve a vital representational role for minority groups.[30] Again, without this additional access point, minority interests should be less well represented in states with direct democracy institutions as legislators become more responsive to majority interests.

So, through both the direct and indirect paths of influence that direct democracy can wield, the impact of the preferences of the majority is magnified. The result of this magnification is a general majoritarian effect on policy outcomes. Empirical research supports this majoritarian impact, showing that states with initiatives are, indeed, more responsive to public opinion than states without direct democracy institutions.[31] This responsiveness may be beneficial to the public in many policy areas, but in states where minority rights are targeted by the majority this induced policy congruence can be problematic. As Gerber and Hug stress, citizen legislation by itself doesn't produce tyrannical outcomes, but coupled with anti-minority public preferences it can be detrimental to the civil rights of minority groups.[32] When the majority preference is at odds with the rights of minority groups, these rights are at risk.

Consequently, there are theoretically compelling reasons to expect that direct citizen legislation would put minority rights in danger—especially when the majority prefers policies that restrict minority rights. However, some scholars contend that direct democracy can avoid the potential negative impacts on minority groups. Gillette argues that the motivations that draw citizens to the voting booth are usually not narrowly focused on a single issue.[33] Thus, voter behavior will be shaped by multiple considerations rather than a singular focus on their ethnic, racial, or other group interests. Empirically, however, it is not clear the extent to which these multiple motivations actually protect against the "tyranny of the majority."

Another potential check on tyrannical outcomes is found in the judicial branch. Ellis notes the significant role of judicial review of citizen-passed legislation.[34] Eule stresses that an active judiciary, serving as a kind of "safety net" for minority rights, is a vital check on the majoritarian tendencies of direct democracy.[35] Some studies find that courts are, indeed, actively reviewing and overturning unconstitutional public initiatives.[36] However, as a relatively passive player in the policy process, it is not apparent the extent to which this institution can protect the rights of minorities against a united majority. In addition, courts may not less willing to take counter-majoritarian action and overturn policies passed directly by "the people" compared with policies adopted by the legislature.[37] Indeed, a recent study finds that judges in direct democracy states are less likely than other judges to vote in favor of gay rights, which suggests that this "safety net" argument may not be empirically supported.[38] Furthermore, overturning citizen legislation is particularly difficult in states that select judges through popular elections. In these states, judges may be reluctant to overturn policies enacted by the same electorate they will have to face in order win reelection.[39]

Despite these potential checks on tyrannical outcomes under direct democracy institutions, theories of filtering through representational democracy, of separated powers, and of the scope of conflict still predict that minority rights would suffer under governmental systems that allow citizen legislation. While the courts and the multiple motivating factors that draw voters to the polls have the potential to check anti-minority policy outcomes, neither directly refutes the theoretical underpinnings that underlie the majoritarian argument. Courts can only act to protect minority rights after a policy has been enacted, and thus the majoritarian tendencies of direct democracy systems should not be altered by an active judiciary. The argument concerning the multiple motivating factors of voters also does not refute the logic of the "tyranny of the majority" argument. Even if some citizens are not motivated to vote by a single issue, this does not mean these voters will not cast their ballot for policies that restrict the rights of minority groups. The motivations of voters also do not address the issue of the indirect effect of direct democracy, where just the threat of citizen legislation creates incentives for legislators to be responsive to the majority.

Thus, the "tyranny of the majority" argument is theoretically sound, and we should expect that states with direct democracy institutions should be more likely to threaten and restrict minority rights. Assuming that the majority of the public will often prefer policies that restrict the minorities, the impact of direct democracy on policy decisions should be to increase responsiveness to these majority preferences. Through both the direct and indirect paths of influence, the total effect of direct democracy should have a negative impact on minority rights.

Whose Rights?

Throughout this discussion, the terms "minorities" and "minority rights" have been used without a clear explanation of exactly to which groups they refer. In the most basic sense, a minority group is any group of citizens defined by some characteristic, such that the group constitutes less than 50 percent of the population in a political system. This broad definition encompasses a huge range of groups distinguished by any number of characteristics. Traditionally, minority groups have been defined by race, ethnicity, and religion. However, other characteristics have also come to define important minority groups in American politics. Indeed, the writings on the factions in *The Federalist Papers* are aimed at groups defined by their social class and economic characteristics. James Madison was concerned with the rights of wealthy elites at the hands of the newly empowered lower class of citizens who comprised the majority of the American population.

At the most abstract level, almost any characteristic can define a minority group. For example, both vegetarians and vegans constitute minority populations in the United States, but dietary choice is not usually considered to be a defining characteristic of minority groups whose civil rights need protecting. Although vegans may be a numerical minority, their distinguishing characteristic is not one that is typically considered in policy and political discussions. A narrower, more practical definition focuses less on the numerical aspects of minorities, and more on their rights *vis-à-vis* a politically dominant majority group. One such approach uses the term "political minorities," which defines minorities as groups that are "subjected to social, political and economic discrimination in society" or have been historically subjected to different legal standards than the majority.[40]

For the purposes of this study, the concept of "political minorities" that focuses on discrimination and political rights is most appropriate. In evaluating whether direct democracy has a negative impact on minority groups, it is necessary to concentrate on the rights of groups that are or have been historically targeted by the majority. It is exactly these groups whose rights are most endangered and have been widely recognized as needing political protection. A more concrete inventory of the characteristics that are most commonly recognized to define political minorities can be found in state and federal civil rights laws and anti-discrimination policies. These widely protected classes include minority groups defined by race, color, religion, ethnicity, and national origin. More recently other groups have also gained recognition as valid "political minorities," including groups defined by their sexual orientation, gender identity, age, gender, and disabilities.

Throughout this book, the analyses focus on political minorities and policy proposals that have an explicit impact on the rights of these groups. While there is certainly a wide range of policies that can affect the interests of minority groups, from environmental policy to tax policy, most do not overtly target the rights of political minorities.[41] Still, there are a non-negligible number of policies that do have a direct and clear impact on the rights of political minorities, like same-sex marriage bans and racial profiling laws. It is exactly these types of policies to which critics of direct democracy are referring in arguing that citizen legislation endangers minority rights.[42] In empirically assessing this argument, it is important that the tests remain focused on these explicit policies that affect the rights of widely recognized political minority groups. In examining these types of policies, I follow the approach of Haider-Markel and his coauthors, concentrating on those issues that fundamentally impact minority rights, and not on those that more tangentially affect minority interests.[43] Thus, the policies under examination here all deal with a minority group's rights in terms of equality under the law, equal opportunity, and individual privacy.

Existing Research

As discussed earlier, there are some theoretical arguments why minority rights are not unduly threatened by citizen legislation, but the most compelling argument against the "tyranny of the majority" critique is based on empirical evidence (or lack thereof). General studies of direct democracy usually concede the potential for civil rights abuses, but also note a lack of empirical evidence to condemn direct democracy institutions as a culprit for impairing minority rights.[44] More recent examinations of empirical record reach similar conclusions. Donovan and Bowler find that statewide initiatives targeting gay rights actually pass at a lower rate than all types of statewide initiatives combined.[45] Hajnal, Gerber, and Louch, in a study of ballot initiatives in California, found that racial and ethnic minorities were no more likely to be on the losing side of an initiative contest than are the majority Anglo voters, and conclude that these minority groups are not being systematically targeted through the initiative process.[46] In a study of direct democracy in Switzerland, where three-quarters of the world's referenda have been held, Frey and Goette found evidence that comparatively few measures restricting minority rights have passed by citizen legislation.[47] In general, these studies conclude that direct democracy institutions are not overly susceptible to anti-minority outcomes.

At the same time, however, there is some empirical research that supports the "tyranny of the majority" argument. In her analysis of anti-minority initiatives and referenda in American states and cities, Barbara Gamble finds that 78 percent of these measures passed.[48] This high passage rate dwarfs the 33 percent rate for the rest of the initiatives and referenda in the sample.[49] Evidence of tyrannical outcomes is also found in several studies of specific anti-minority policies, such as Official English language measures, affirmative action bans, and anti-gay rights policies.[50]

In all, the extant literature presents a decidedly mixed picture of the impact of direct democracy institutions on minority rights. A shortcoming of most of this research, regardless of which side of the debate it supports, is that it only examines measures considered and passed through citizen legislation while omitting traditional legislation from the analyses.[51] As discussed earlier, direct democracy institutions have both direct effects on policy decisions through citizen legislation, as well as indirect effects by influencing legislators' behavior. In order to understand the full impact of direct democracy institutions on minority rights, it is necessary to examine both paths of influence and include citizen legislation as well as traditional legislation in the study.

Another limitation of the existing research is also rooted in the singular focus on policies passed by citizen legislation. At its heart, the "tyranny of the majority" argument is a comparative one. James Madison advocates for a representative form of government than can provide a "cure" for the ills of factions, whereas pure democracy is unable to cope with these issues.[52] In other words, he argues that representative government can better protect the rights of minorities than a pure democracy. Thus, the most direct test of this argument would be to compare policy decisions in direct democracy governments with those produced by representative governments. If direct democracy institutions do endanger minority rights, then governments with these institutions should be more likely to pass anti-minority policies than those governments that have purely representative systems.

In order to directly test this comparative argument, while also accounting for both the direct and indirect impacts of direct democracy, it is necessary to explore the determinants of the adoption of all types of anti-minority policies, regardless of the legislative vehicle that passes them, in both direct democracy and non-direct democracy states. The few studies that have used a similar research design have found that direct democracy does contribute to negative outcomes for minority groups. In studies of state adoptions of Official English language measures, Schildkraut and Preuhs find that initiative states are more likely to adopt as the number of foreign-born population increases.[53] Non-initiative states, meanwhile, show decreasing likelihoods of adoption as the foreign-born population in the states increase. These findings are consistent with the theory that representative governments provide a filtering and representational function that helps to protect minority rights. On the other hand, direct democracy provides a way to circumvent these processes, leading to more majoritarian policy outcomes.

The studies of Official English laws certainly provide evidence of the potential detrimental effects of direct democracy, but these effects are contingent on a rising "threat-level" posed by the foreign-born population. Yet, it is not clear how well this finding generalizes to other issue areas. These studies examine the rights of linguistic and ethnic minorities. Do these results extend to other types of minorities (i.e., based on race or sexual orientation)? Are less dynamic populations of minority groups also endangered by direct democracy institutions? How does direct democracy impact the adoption of policies that explicitly protect minority rights?

Goals and Plan of the Book

The goal of this book is to directly and systematically test whether minority rights are less protected in states with direct democracy institutions, and to provide a better understanding of the impact that these institutions have on minority groups. The book is organized into three analytic studies. Chapter 2 focuses on the adoption of specific, contemporary anti-minority policies in the American states. In this analysis, I ask whether direct democracy states are more likely to adopt these policies than states without direct democracy institutions. The third chapter examines individual anti-minority policy proposals, asking whether the filtering mechanisms of representative democracy are reducing the likelihood that these proposals become law. While these first two studies focus on anti-minority policies, Chapter 4 takes a contrasting perspective by asking whether direct democracy also influences the consideration of policy proposals that would protect or enhance minority rights. Similar in design to the first set of analyses, this chapter examines specific contemporary policies that protect minority rights. Together these three analyses provide a more complete picture of how direct democracy affects the rights of political minorities in the American states.

2

DIRECT DEMOCRACY AND THE DIFFUSION OF ANTI-MINORITY POLICIES

One way to evaluate the "tyranny of the majority" theory is to examine the diffusion of anti-minority policies across the American states. If direct democracy does endanger minority rights, then states with ballot initiatives and referenda should be more likely and quicker to adopt an anti-minority policy than states without direct democracy institutions. With the ability to circumvent the representational filters of traditional democratic government, a united majority should be better able to enact their preferred policy with little resistance from minority groups.

In this chapter, I examine the spread of three contemporary anti-minority policies to provide answers to the following question: Are direct democracy states more likely than non-initiative states to adopt a specific anti-minority? The three policies under examination here are same-sex marriage bans, Official English laws, and affirmative action bans. While the normative nature of these policies is certainly open to debate, they all clearly target a political minority group and restrict their rights in some way. In addition, each of these three policies targets different political minorities, allowing for a more general understanding of how minority groups are affected by direct democracy; same-sex marriage bans target homosexuals, Official English laws target speakers of foreign languages (usually of Hispanic or Asian descent), and affirmative action bans broadly target racial and ethnic minorities.

Same-Sex Marriage Bans

Same-sex marriage in the United States has been arguably the most visible issue in the gay rights movement in recent years.[1] While same-sex marriage has been part of the gay rights debate since same-sex couples in Wisconsin and Minnesota were denied the right to marry in 1971, the issue did not shift from the courts to the legislatures until the 1990s. Early court rulings refused to recognize same-sex marriage, but in the absence of laws that explicitly banned gay marriage judicial decisions often relied on biblical references.[2]

It was not until 1993, when the Hawaii Supreme Court ruled in *Baehr v. Lewin* that prohibiting same-sex couples from marrying violates the Hawaii Constitution's ban on sex discrimination, that the issue entered the legislative arena and attracted national attention. Alarmed by the prospect of state recognition of same-sex marriages, opponents moved to pass laws that banned recognition of gay marriages and similar unions. At first these efforts bore little success, but when the federal government enacted the Defense of Marriage Act (DOMA) in 1996 the states soon followed in passing their own versions of the law. A significant feature of the DOMA is that it exempts state marriage laws from the "full faith and credit" clause of the U.S. Constitution. States are constitutionally required to recognize legal contracts from other states, but the passage of the DOMA excused states from recognizing marriages issued by other states. Prior to the DOMA, a state like Utah, which banned same-sex marriage in 1995, would nonetheless be required to recognize same-sex marriages conducted in other states where these contracts were legal.

Following the passage of the DOMA, states across the country began considering and adopting same-sex marriage bans of their own. From 1995 to 2008, forty-three states adopted laws prohibiting recognition of same-sex marriages. Figure 2.1 shows the timing of the states' initial adoptions of same-sex marriage bans over this time period.[3] Utah led the way in 1995 and sixteen states enacted bans the next year. Nine more states followed in 1997. After the initial rush of legislation, the flow of statutes barring recognition of gay marriage slowed. This pattern of yearly adoptions, as well as the cumulative adoption pattern (both shown in Figure 2.1), fits nicely with traditional models of the diffusion of innovation.[4] Diffusion of innovation is the process by which states adopt new policies or programs. Policy innovations often spread to other states through a variety of external and internal factors, producing a distinctive pattern of cumulative adoptions.[5] The cumulative adoption line in Figure 2.1 shows this pattern of an "S-shaped" curve where a few early adopters (in this case, just Utah) are followed by a flurry of adoptions in the next couple of years as state policymakers emulate and take cues from one another. The line then flattens as the last few states adopt their own policies.

Although new state adoptions slowed to a standstill by 2001, same-sex marriage soon returned to the national agenda following several events in 2003 and 2004 relevant to the gay rights debate. In 2003, the U.S. Supreme Court, in *Lawrence v. Texas*, ruled that all thirteen remaining state sodomy laws were unconstitutional. That same year, the Massachusetts Supreme Court issued the first of a series of decisions ruling that the state constitution mandates marriage equality. The next

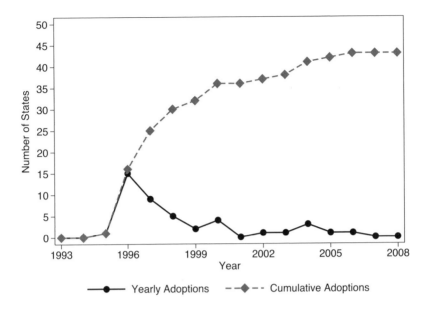

FIGURE 2.1 Initial State Adoptions of Same-Sex Marriage Bans, 1993–2008

year several local officials began actively pursuing recognition of same-sex marriages. San Francisco Mayor Gavin Newsom led this movement, granting over 4,000 same-sex marriage licenses. Local officials in New Mexico, New York, Oregon, and Washington soon followed suit. With all the increased activism and swell of media attention, the debate over same-sex marriage spurred a backlash, and new legislative efforts were soon undertaken. Ballots in thirteen states in 2004 included proposed bans on the recognition of gay marriage. All thirteen passed with at least of 56 percent of the vote.

On the one hand, the 2004 elections provide a good example illustrating the "tyranny of the majority" theory: Thirteen anti-minority policies were proposed and passed despite strong resistance from the targeted minority.[6] On the other hand, only two of these states were enacting their initial same-sex marriage ban, and thirty-eight states before them had already adopted similar policies. Indeed, most same-sex marriage bans have been enacted with traditional legislation (see Figure 2.2). So what exactly has been the role of direct democracy in the adoption of same-sex marriage bans in the American states?

Table 2.1 sheds some light on this question, showing all proposals to ban same-sex marriage that have been placed on statewide ballots. Despite all the media attention to the thirteen states with bans on the ballot in 2004, only Ohio and Oregon were enacting their initial laws against same-sex marriage. The other

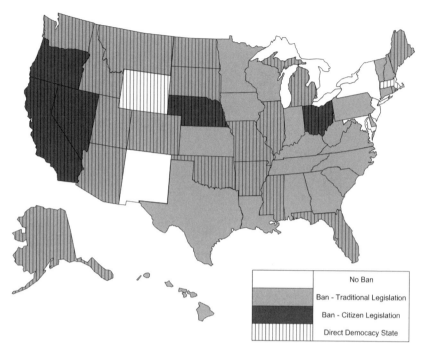

FIGURE 2.2 Initial State Same-Sex Marriage Bans, 1993–2008

eleven states with same-sex marriage ban proposals on their ballot in 2004 were reinforcing previously passed statutes with constitutional amendments.[7] In all, only five states used direct democracy institutions as vehicle to enact their initial prohibitions. The use of direct democracy by fifteen other states reinforced existing policy, but did not fundamentally alter it. In many cases these reinforcing policies were enacted without circumventing the legislature, and only utilized direct democracy as a ratification requirement to amend their constitution. The majority of these policies were not initiated directly by citizens. Judging from the frequency with which citizen legislation has been used to ban same-sex marriage, it seems as if direct democracy may not have played a large role in states adopting these policies.

While citizen legislation only makes up less than 12 percent of the initial prohibitions of same-sex marriage in the states, only one ballot measure addressing this issue has failed to pass. Though Arizona's initiative to amend its constitution barely lost with 48.2 percent of the vote in 2006, a legislative constitutional amendment did pass in 2008 with 56.2 percent support. On average, ballot measures to ban same-sex marriage have garnered 67 percent of the vote. So even though ballot initiatives have not been the most oft-used vehicle to adopt same-sex marriage bans, they have been enormously successful when employed.

TABLE 2.1 Citizen Legislation Proposing to Ban Same-Sex Marriage, 1995–2008

State	Year	Type of ban	Vote %	Initial ban?
Alaska	1998	Constitutional amendment	68.1	
Arizona	2006	Constitutional amendment	48.2	
California[a]	2000	Statute	61.4	▲
California[a]	2008	Constitutional amendment	52.3	▲
Colorado	2006	Constitutional amendment	55.0	
Florida	2006	Constitutional amendment	61.9	
Nebraska	2000	Constitutional amendment	70.0	▲
Nevada[b]	2000	Constitutional amendment	70.0	▲
Nevada[b]	2002	Constitutional amendment	66.9	▲
Arkansas	2004	Constitutional amendment	75.0	
Georgia	2004	Constitutional amendment	76.2	
Kentucky	2004	Constitutional Amendment	74.6	
Louisiana	2004	Constitutional amendment	78.0	
Michigan	2004	Constitutional amendment	58.6	
Mississippi	2004	Constitutional amendment	86.0	
Missouri	2004	Constitutional amendment	70.7	
Montana	2004	Constitutional amendment	66.6	
North Dakota	2004	Constitutional amendment	73.2	
Ohio	2004	Constitutional amendment	61.7	▲
Oklahoma	2004	Constitutional amendment	75.6	
Oregon	2004	Constitutional amendment	56.6	▲
Utah	2004	Constitutional amendment	65.9	

Notes:
a California adopted its initial ban in 2000, but it was overturned by the state supreme court in 2008. Subsequently, an initiative to amend the constitution to reinstate the ban was passed later that year.
b Nevada requires constitutional amendments to pass through the public initiative process twice before it becomes law.

This brief review of the politics of same-sex marriage policies in the American states presents a mixed picture of the role of the direct impact of direct democracy in this policy area. On the one hand, most states have prohibited same-sex marriage through traditional legislative means. Even when citizen legislation is used, it tends to reinforce existing policy rather than initiating the policy change in the first place. On the other hand, anti-gay marriage initiatives have passed nearly 97 percent of the time. Once on the ballot, it appears that the minority gay population in the state has virtually no chance of defeating these proposals.

Event History Analysis

To get a better grasp on the effect of citizen legislation on a state's propensity to adopt same-sex marriage bans, it is necessary to move beyond the direct impact of direct democracy and assess the indirect impacts as well. By examining policy decisions from both citizen legislation (the direct effect) and traditional legislation (the indirect effect), I can effectively assess the total impact of direct democracy institutions. To that end, this analysis uses an event history approach to examine state adoptions. Event history modeling, alternatively known as survival or hazard analysis, is a good way answer the following question: Given that a state has not previously adopted a gay marriage ban, what is the probability that it will do so in a given year?

To address this question, yearly data were collected on forty-nine states from 1994 (following Hawaii's *Baehr v. Lewin* ruling in 1993) to 2006.[8] These data have two important features that make event history analysis particularly appropriate here. First, since some states had not yet adopted same-sex marriage bans by 2006, but certainly have the potential to do so in the following years, the data is right-censored. Static regression analyses generally do not differentiate between right-censored and uncensored observations, which could lead to biased estimates of the impact of the independent variables. Another important characteristic of the data is its temporality. With yearly data, there are defined discrete time periods rather than continuous temporality.

Cox proportional hazards analysis is well suited to deal with this dynamic, right-censored, discrete data. As with all event history models, it addresses the issues of bias related to right-censoring. In addition, it allows for the analysis of independent variables without any assumptions about the distribution of the baseline hazard rate. Most event history models account for the dynamic nature of the data by assuming a particular form of an underlying propensity for the event to occur, often exponentially or linearly increasing over time. The baseline hazard rate in the Cox model, however, is unspecified and flexible. Since this study is primarily focused on the impact of direct democracy institutions while controlling for several other factors, and not on the duration dependency of state adoptions, the Cox model is particularly appropriate here. Additionally, since I use an exact-discrete approximation for tied cases (multiple adoptions in a year), the Cox models presented here are equivalent to conditional logistic regression models or a fixed-effects model that can make interpreting the results more straightforward.[9]

The dependent variable in this study is a binary indicator of whether a state adopted its initial same-sex marriage ban in a given year—zero in years when a state does not adopt a ban and one in the year in which a state does adopt the policy. I do not differentiate between traditional legislation and citizen legislation, or between statutes and constitution amendments. The focus here is on the propensity of states to adopt policies that ban same-sex marriage, not the process by which the policy is enacted. Once a state adopts its initial same-sex marriage ban, it drops out of the analysis. I confine the analysis to include only the initial same-sex marriage ban, since this is the policy outcome that functions to restrict gay rights. Subsequent reinforcements, often in the form of a constitutional amendment, simply make the existing policy harder to overturn, but generally do not drastically alter the content of the policy.

The main explanatory variable for this study measures a state's direct democracy institutions. The most straight-forward way to measure direct democracy is a dichotomous variable indicating whether the state has direct democracy institutions. While this measure has intuitive appeal in its simple interpretation, it cannot account for the variation in the arrangements of the state direct democracy institutions described in the previous chapter. Thus, I also employ an alternative measure of direct democracy that distinguishes between these various arrangements.

The variations in how states arrange their direct democracy institutions can be assessed in multiple ways (see Table 2.2). One approach creates measures of legislative insulation and qualification difficulty.[10] The Legislative Insulation Index ranges from zero to nine, and gauges the extent to which the legislature is isolated from the effects of citizen legislation. It accounts for whether the legislature can modify citizen legislative outcomes, how difficult the modification process is, and whether there are subject limits to citizen legislation (among other factors). California is the least insulated, with institutional characteristics like the inability to modify initiatives, no fiscal restrictions on initiatives, and no indirect initiatives. The qualification index, ranging from zero to six, measures how difficult it is to qualify for the ballot in each state. Qualification restrictions include geographic distribution of signature requirements, the proportion of signature required, and substantive subject matter restrictions (among others). Oregon tops the qualification index list with relatively minimal requirements to place a proposal on the ballot.

Another way to account for the differences in the states' direct democracy institutions is the frequency of initiative use.[11] States that use direct democracy more often tend to have easier qualification rules and less legislative modification.[12] Hence, direct democracy should have a larger impact on policy decisions in states that use initiatives more often. For this analysis and all subsequent ones, initiative use is operationalized as the number of initiatives and referenda placed on the ballot during the time period under examination.

Since each of these variables measures direct democracy institutions in a different way, it is not surprising that they are all highly correlated with one another. To avoid statistical problems such as multicollinearity, while at the same time accounting for all the aspects of direct democracy institutions that are measured with each of the variables, I create a single measure using a principal components analysis (PCA) of the Legislative Insulation Index, the Qualification Difficulty Index, and the natural log of initiative use. In addition to avoiding statistical problems associated with the high correlations of these three measures, this approach also allows for a relatively parsimonious test of the impact of direct democracy on policy adoption while guarding against spurious results that might plague a binary measure. The first component produced from the PCA accounts

TABLE 2.2 Measures of Direct Democracy

State	Legislative Insulation Index*	Qualification Difficulty Index*	Initiative use, 1994–2008	Direct Democracy impact
Wyoming	1	1	5	1.043
Mississippi	3	2	2	1.377
Illinois	5	3	0	1.792
Maine	2	3	19	2.241
Alaska	4	2	24	2.483
Massachusetts	2	4	24	2.580
Nebraska	4	3	16	2.590
Utah	6	4	5	2.835
Missouri	4	4	17	2.867
Florida	5	3	20	2.877
Oklahoma	6	4	6	2.901
Nevada	5	3	27	2.986
Montana	4	4	24	2.992
Ohio	4	5	14	3.051
Idaho	6	5	11	3.375
South Dakota	6	5	20	3.592
Washington	6	4	46	3.639
Michigan	7	5	15	3.693
Arkansas	8	5	9	3.714
Arizona	7	4	36	3.756
North Dakota	7	6	16	3.971
Colorado	7	6	50	4.383
Oregon	7	7	87	4.839
California	9	6	86	4.992

Notes:
The twenty-six states without direct democracy institutions (not shown here) have a score of zero on all measures.
* Based on Shaun Bowler, and Todd Donovan, 2004. "Measuring the Effects of Direct Democracy on State Policy: Not All Initiatives are Created Equal." *State Politics and Policy Quarterly* 4:345–63. Higher scores indicate less insulation and less qualification difficulty (i.e., fewer restrictions on direct democracy).

for nearly 95 percent of the variance of these three variables. The three measures were then combined, weighted by the eigenvectors from the first component.[13] The resultant Direct Democracy Impact score ranges from zero for non–direct democracy states to nearly five for California (see Table 2.2). The average score for direct democracy states is just over three. Higher scores indicate that direct democracy should have more of an impact on policy outcomes, and thus should be more likely to adopt a same-sex marriage ban.

In addition to the measures of direct democracy, the analyses also account for a host of other determinants of state policy adoption. General public opinion is accounted for using the citizen ideology measure developed by Berry, Ringquist, Fording, and Hanson.[14] Based on the ideologies of elected officials and their electoral support, higher scores indicate more liberal citizen ideologies or public moods. States with lower, more conservative, ideology scores should be more likely to adopt same-sex marriage bans.[15]

The models include two variables designed to gauge the strength of organized interests on each side of this issue. Generally, advocacy for DOMA legislation and same-sex marriage bans stems from the conservative Christian community.[16] Since this movement is led by citizen organizations, it is possible to gauge the membership resources available in a state to conservative Christian groups by a count of the evangelical population in each state provided by the Association of Statisticians of American Religious Bodies.[17] The rate of evangelicals in a state population should be a good indicator of the strength of the conservative Christian movement in that state. States with higher rates of evangelical Christian membership should have a higher likelihood of adopting same-sex marriage bans. The strength of gay rights organizations is measured in a similar manner. A state's gay population is based on estimates of the percentage of coupled households that are same-sex partner households from the 2000 Census.[18] States with higher percentages of same-sex partner households should be less likely to adopt a same-sex marriage ban.

To control for partisan influences on state policymaking, the analyses include a variable indicating unified Republican control of the state government and another indicating unified Democratic control of the state government. Since Republicans tend to be more ideologically conservative and enjoy support from the conservative Christian community, Republican governments should be more likely than either Democratic or divided governments to enact same-sex marriage bans. Jointly, these two party control variables also account for the differences between unified and divided government. All things equal, unified governments should be more likely than divided governments to pass any type of policy. Since party control is already accounted for, the models also include a folded Ranney index to control for party competition.[19] Given the broad popular support for same-sex marriage bans, states with higher party competition should be more likely to adopt these measures as parties compete for public support and electoral success.

The influence of geographic policy diffusion is assessed with the proportion of adjacent states that have passed same-sex marriage bans. The diffusion literature suggests that a state will be more likely to pass new policies when neighboring states have already passed those policies.[20] However, in the case of same-sex marriage bans, the geographic diffusion may have an opposite effect. One of the key aspects of the federal DOMA is that it allows states to ignore marriages from other states. If all the surrounding states have already banned same-sex marriage there may be less incentive for a state to adopt a gay marriage ban of its own.

The models also include several indicators of the legal environment pertaining to gay rights in each state.[21] In particular, there are controls for whether a state

has the following laws: a civil union or domestic partnership statute, any criminal-
ization of sodomy, a nondiscrimination law that includes sexual preference, or
statutory language that predates the contemporary debate over same-sex marriage
that defines marriage as only between a man and woman.[22] Civil unions and legally
recognized domestic partnerships are often viewed as equivalent substitutes to
marriage, so states with these laws may be more likely to adopt a same-sex marriage
ban. For example, Connecticut's 2005 civil union bill was signed into law
by Governor Jodi Rell only after an amendment defining marriage as between
a man and woman was added. The presence of sodomy laws, an indicator of legal
environments that are hostile towards gay rights, should also increase the
likelihood of adopting a same-sex marriage ban. Nondiscrimination laws that
include sexual orientation, meanwhile, should decrease the likelihood of enacting
a ban since these laws are indicative of a more tolerant legal environment. Finally,
a few states have statutory language enacted well before the contemporary debate
that describes marriage in such way that indicates that it is a heterosexual
arrangement. For example, prior to passing a constitutional amendment in 2006,
Wisconsin law already stated that "marriage is a legal relationship between two
equal persons, a husband and wife, who owe to each other mutual responsibility
and support."[23] This type of language could understandably be interpreted as
defining marriage as only between a man and woman. Thus, these states should
be less likely to adopt a new same-sex marriage ban.

The final three control variables are demographic variables. Based on Publius'
treatment of the majority faction problem and the contention that majorities could
be constrained by the "enlargement of the orbit," larger (more populous) states
should be less likely to adopt measures that restrict minority rights.[24] The next
demographic control gauges the level of educational attainment in a state as
measured by the percent of the population over twenty-five years old with at
least a bachelor's degree. Higher levels of education have been shown to be
consistent determinants of tolerance of minority groups.[25] The final demographic
control is the percent of a state's population that is black. Popular accounts of
gay rights issues have suggested that race may play a role in attitudes toward
homosexuals, but scholarly examinations have not found this to be the case.[26]
Rather, religiosity, which can be easily entangled with race, is the driving force
behind attitudes towards gay rights and homosexuality.[27]

As discussed earlier, one advantage of the Cox proportional hazards model is
its assumption that time dependency has an arbitrary form. This assumption allows
the baseline hazard to vary over time. Due to this aspect of the model, indicators
of spurring events or other dichotomous measures of temporality cannot be
included. Still, it is reasonable to expect that the court decisions in 2003 and
2004, and the willingness of local officials to grant same-sex marriage licenses in
2004, would spur states to adopt bans. These temporal affects are evident when
examining the estimated hazard functions from the Cox model. Figure 2.3 shows
the hazard functions of states with direct democracy and states without direct

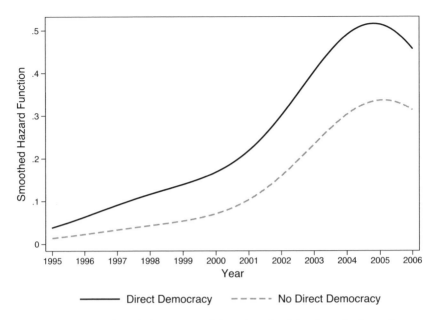

FIGURE 2.3 Estimated Underlying Hazard Functions for Adoption of a Same-Sex Marriage Ban

democracy, and a considerable increase in the hazard rate is clearly visible during and immediately following this time period, suggesting that these judicial events did have an effect on all states' propensity to adopt same-sex marriage bans.

The full results from the Cox proportional hazards analysis are shown in Table 2.3. The coefficients can be interpreted similarly to conditional logistic regression coefficients, as the effect that a one unit change in the independent variable has on the log-odds of a state adopting a same-sex marriage ban in a particular year. Consequently, initial interpretations of the results should focus on the direction of the coefficient and its statistical significance. Alternatively, the magnitude of the coefficients can be assessed by converting them to hazard ratios (odds ratios) that show the impact of the variable on the odds of the event occurring.

The estimation results clearly and consistently support the "tyranny of the majority" argument. The first model, using the simple indicator of direct democracy institutions, shows that direct democracy states are significantly more likely than non-direct democracy states to adopt a same-sex marriage ban in a given year. Converting the coefficients to hazard ratios reveals that the odds of adopting this policy are nearly three times higher in direct democracy states compared with other states.

The second model also supports the "tyranny of the majority" argument. Furthermore, the coefficient on the Direct Democracy Impact variable shows how variations in institutional arrangements of direct democracy affect policy

TABLE 2.3 State Adoptions of Same-Sex Marriage Bans, 1994–2006

	(1)		(2)	
Variable	*Coefficient*	*p-value*	*Coefficient*	*p-value*
Direct democracy [+]	**1.067**	**(0.014)**	—	—
Direct Democracy Impact [+]	—	—	**0.436**	**(0.002)**
Citizen ideology [–]	−0.013	(0.297)	−0.018	(0.238)
Evangelical rate [+]	**0.073**	**(0.006)**	**0.069**	**(0.009)**
Same-sex households [–]	**−2.462**	**(0.050)**	**−2.829**	**(0.032)**
Republican government [+]	**2.266**	**(0.001)**	**2.317**	**(0.001)**
Democratic government	**1.800**	**(0.007)**	**1.975**	**(0.004)**
Party competition [+]	**13.456**	**(0.000)**	**13.973**	**(0.000)**
Bordering states w/bans	**−3.076**	**(0.001)**	**−3.529**	**(0.000)**
Civil unions or partnerships [+]	**1.752**	**(0.052)**	**1.709**	**(0.059)**
Sodomy law [+]	**1.846**	**(0.004)**	**2.034**	**(0.003)**
Nondiscrimination law [–]	−0.657	(0.181)	−0.359	(0.309)
Predating language [–]	**−2.961**	**(0.003)**	**−2.112**	**(0.021)**
Population (log) [–]	**−0.478**	**(0.041)**	**−0.476**	**(0.038)**
Educational attainment [–]	**−0.095**	**(0.084)**	**−0.121**	**(0.037)**
Percent black [+]	−0.012	(0.708)	0.001	(0.966)
Observations	309		309	
Log Likelihood	−93.816		−91.751	

Notes: *p*-values in parentheses (one-tailed tests where appropriate); expected direction of coefficient in brackets; *p*<0.1 in bold.

adoption. The statistically significant, positive coefficient clearly shows that direct democracy states (with an impact score greater than zero) are more likely to adopt a same-sex marriage ban than non-direct democracy states (with an impact score of zero). The hazard ratios reveal that the odds of passing a same-sex marriage ban in a state with a mean score on the Direct Democracy Impact measure are nearly four times higher than in a non-direct democracy state. Moreover, direct democracy states with high-impact institutional arrangements are significantly more likely than other direct democracy states to adopt this anti-minority policy. The odds of a high-impact direct democracy state, like California, adopting this anti-minority policy are over seven times higher than a low-impact direct democracy state, such as Wyoming. Put another way, same-sex marriage bans are more likely to be passed in states that use citizen legislation more often, where it is relatively easy to qualify a proposal for the ballot, and where the legislature is less insulated from direct democracy.

Beyond the impact of direct democracy, the models reveal several other significant factors influencing the diffusion of same-sex marriage bans. The interest group resource coefficients are both statistically significant, showing that increased organizational resources for conservation Christian groups increases the likelihood of adoption while an increase in organization resources for gay right groups decreases the likelihood of adoption. The analyses do not find partisan differences in the propensity to adopt same-sex marriage bans between Republican and Democratic governments, but do show that unified control of government makes policy adoption significantly more likely than divided government. Joint tests of the party control variables confirm this interpretation. Given the wide-spread support for same-sex marriage bans, it is not surprising that both parties would move to enact these popular policies. Party competition also has a positive impact. While this may seem to contradict the previous result, consider that a state can be very narrowly controlled by one party and still have high levels of party competition. In this case, party competition creates incentives for both parties to cater to the policy preferences of large majorities and enact popular policies like same-sex marriage bans.

Somewhat surprisingly, the geographic diffusion variable has a negative coefficient. As the proportion of neighboring states with same-sex marriage bans increases, the likelihood of a state adopting its own ban actually tends to decrease. As discussed earlier, the federal DOMA excludes marriage laws from the "full faith and credit" clause that forces states to recognize contracts made in other states. This exclusion creates a motivation for states that view the recognition of same-sex marriages granted in other states as a realistic "threat" to pass their own bans. When most of the surrounding states have already banned same-sex marriage, the "threat" of same-sex marriages from other states may be diminished and the incentive to pass their own policies is lower.

Other control variables perform as expected. A legal climate in which sodomy is criminalized significantly increases the odds of that state adopting a same sex marriage ban. States with existing statutory language that can be interpreted to define marriage as only between a man and woman are less likely to adopt a redundant law banning same-sex marriage. The substitutive effect of civil union and domestic partnership policies is marginally significant in most of the models. Finally, states with larger and more educated populations tend to be less likely to adopt same-sex marriage bans.

In all, the results of this analysis consistently support the hypothesis that direct democracy states are more likely to adopt an anti-minority policy like a same-sex marriage ban than states with purely representative democratic governments. While ballot initiatives have only been utilized by five states to enact their initial bans on same-sex marriage, the effect of direct democracy institutions seems to be far more pervasive. This direct effect of direct democracy institutions is also supplemented by an indirect effect. The presence of direct democracy institutions increases the likelihood that a state government will adopt a same-sex marriage ban.

Official English

The evidence presented in the previous section strongly supports the critique that direct democracy endangers minority rights. However, the case of same-sex marriage policy may be difficult to generalize to all anti-minority policies. The adoption of same-sex marriage bans from 1995 to 2006 was supported by large majorities in most states during this time period and the policy has been passed by near every state in the union. So how will this critique hold up under different circumstances? In this section, I examine another contemporary minority rights issue: Official English. These policies, also known as English Only laws, declare English to be an official state language and require that government services, such as licensing and elections, only be conducted in English. Whereas same-sex marriage bans have been adopted in almost every state, English is the official state language of just over half of the states. Official English policies directly target Limited English Proficient (LEP) speakers, but also adversely affect large minority groups based on ethnicity and race rather than sexual orientation. Despite these differences, both issues target minority groups, and therefore should be more likely to be adopted in states that have direct democracy institutions. Like the previous analysis, this section will take an event history approach to examine the effect of direct democracy institutions on the likelihood of adopting this anti-minority policy while controlling for the myriad of other determinants of policy adoption.

Although English has been the most dominant and common language in the country, the United States has never had an official language. While there is evidence that the founding fathers considered the role of language in the formation of the new republic, the language debate did not produce an official declaration of a national language.[28] This seems to reflect the conclusion that an official language was not necessary for the fledgling nation. English was the *de facto* language of government and the vast majority of commerce, so it was assumed that it would continue to be the dominant language. At the same time, the country was populated by a diverse array of non-English-speaking immigrants whose support was crucial to the new democracy.[29] Indeed, many of the important political documents of the time, like the Articles of Confederation and *The Federalist Papers*, were printed in multiple languages, while the Constitution itself remained silent on the question of language.[30]

It was not until the twentieth century that American governments began to address the issue of an official language. The first major spurt of language legislation was aimed mainly at restricting the German language during and immediately following World War I. While this era saw the introduction of "liberty cabbage" instead of sauerkraut and "Salisbury steak" instead of hamburger, widespread language legislation did not flourish until the 1980s.[31] Two events in the 1970s precipitated the Official English movement in the following decade. In 1974, the U.S. Supreme Court ruled in *Lau v. Nichols* that schools that did not provide non-English-speaking students the opportunity to "participate meaningfully" were in violation of the 1964 Civil Rights Act, amounting to discrimination based on national origin. In 1975, language provisions were added to the Voting Rights Act of 1965 that required bilingual ballots in communities where non-English speakers accounted for at least 5 percent of the population. Congress concluded that English Only ballots, coupled with English Only education, were excluding language and ethnic minorities from democratic participation.[32] Together these events were perceived to be a national policy of language pluralism.

In a backlash to these policies and to the changing demographic makeup of the country, the contemporary Official English movement was born. It formally began with the introduction of a proposed constitutional amendment to designate English as the sole official language of the United States by Senator S. I. Hayakawa (R–CA) in 1981. This amendment ultimately failed, but similar amendments have been introduced to Congress every year since then. Senator Hayakawa also co-founded the group U.S. English in 1983 to lead the Official English movement.[33] While Official English proposals have not been able to attract much support at the federal level, groups like U.S. English have been more successful at the state level.

Though most state Official English policies are products of the contemporary English Only movement, five states do have policies that predate this period. These older policies, however, tend to be more symbolic than functional. Louisiana, with its French heritage, officially adopted English as its language of record when it joined the Union in 1812, but retained its francophone rights as well. In the courts and the legislature most business was conducted bilingually, reflecting the widespread use of French in Louisiana throughout the nineteenth century. Nebraska and Illinois were the next states to adopt an official state language policy in the 1920s. In an era of "nativism" and "wartime hysteria," when anti-foreign and specifically anti-German sentiment was at its peak in America, Nebraska amended its constitution in 1920 to declare English the official state language.[34] Illinois followed suit three years later, adopting "American" as its official language. The official language was later changed to English in 1969. Like Louisiana's language policy, the last two states to adopt English as an official language prior to the contemporary movement also adopted measures that amounted to bilingual or pluralist policies. Massachusetts required English proficiency as a requirement for political participation in 1975, but still maintained a policy of bilingual education for immigrant children. Hawaii's policy, enacted in 1978, is officially bilingual, recognizing both English and Hawaiian as the official state languages.

At the state level, the contemporary Official English movement started with Virginia's adoption of its language law in 1981. In what Tatalovich calls "nativism reborn," this movement has been propelled by negative responses to the growing Spanish-speaking population in the United States.[35] Figure 2.4 shows the timing of the contemporary adoptions of Official English, revealing two periods of policy adoption, marked by S-shaped curves in the cumulative adoption line. First, the

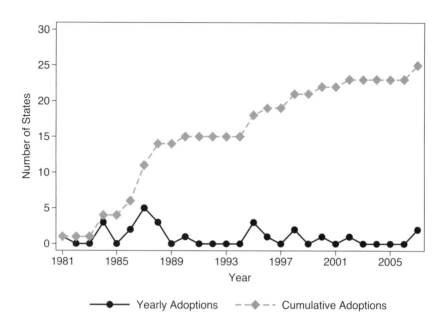

FIGURE 2.4 State Adoptions of Official English, 1981–2007

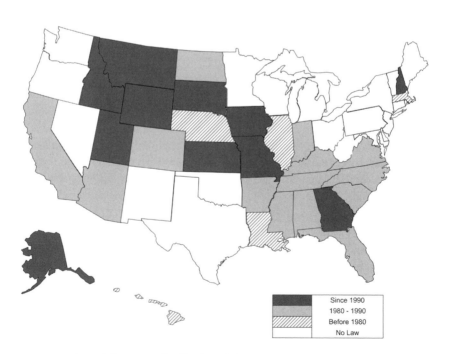

FIGURE 2.5 State Adoptions of Official English Policies, 1981–2007

TABLE 2.4 English Only Ballot Measures, 1980–2008

Official English measures			
State	Year	Type of law	Vote for
Alaska	1998	Statute	68.6%
Arizona★	1988	Amendment	50.5%
Arizona★	2006	Amendment	74.2%
California	1986	Amendment	73.3%
Colorado	1988	Amendment	61.2%
Missouri★★	2008	Amendment	85.8%
Florida	1988	Statute	84.0%
Utah	2000	Statute	67.2%
Other language policies			
State	Year	Subject of law	Vote for
Arizona	2000	Education	63.0%
California	1984	Voting	70.7%
California	1998	Education	60.9%
Colorado	2002	Education	44.6%
Massachusetts	2002	Education	68.0%
Oregon	2008	Education	43.6%

Notes:

★   Arizona's initial amendment was overturned in 1998.

★★ Missouri passed a constitutional amendment reinforcing their existing statutory Official English law.

mid-1980s witnessed a spike in adoptions, with fifteen states enacting their policies by the end of the decade. A lull in the diffusion of Official English followed until the mid-1990s. From 1995 to 2002, though, a second wave of adoptions occurred, with eight more states declaring English as the official state language.

By 2007, twenty-nine states had declared English to be the official state language. Figure 2.5 shows all the states that have an official language. Most of these adoptions occurred after 1980 during the modern Official English movement and have substantive impact on the state government's use of language in its programs. By contrast, the five states that adopted an official language prior to 1980 have more symbolic language policies, as described earlier.

Like same-sex marriage bans, most Official English laws have been passed through traditional legislation. Table 2.4 shows the English Only ballot measures —including Official English laws as well as more narrowly tailored language restrictions—considered in the states since 1980. Of the twenty-five states that have adopted an Official English policy, only six used citizen legislation to achieve this outcome. The pattern of Official English adoptions is also similar to the same-sex marriage bans in terms of its success. Each of the six states using citizen legislation passed the measure; usually by a wide margin. Other English Only policies that have addressed education and voting issues have also met with comparable success. The exceptions are two proposals to move from bilingual education to English immersion education in Colorado and Oregon. Again, in examining only the outcomes from citizen legislation, it looks as if direct democracy may not increase the likelihood of a state adopting Official English. As shown in the previous section, though, only focusing outcomes of citizen legislation can be misleading.

Event History Analysis

To fully assess the impact of direct democracy on the adoption of Official English laws it is necessary to account for both the direct and indirect effects by examining policy decisions from both citizen legislation and traditional legislation. To that end, this analysis follows the event history approach from the preceding section to answer the question: Given that a state has not adopted an Official English policy in previous years, what is the probability that it will do so in that year?

In the case of Official English, data has been collected on forty-five states from 1981 to 2007.[36] The analysis begins in 1981, because this is the year Virginia adopted its Official English law. This adoption was the first language policy enacted in response to a perceived federal policy of language pluralism.[37] It was in 1981 also that Sen. Hayakawa (R-CA) first proposed an Official English amendment to the Constitution, propelling the issue to the national stage. As with the same-sex marriage ban analysis, this data is yearly and right-censored. As such, a Cox proportion hazards model that uses the exact discrete method for ties is well suited to analyze this policy as well.

The dependent variable for this analysis is an indicator of whether or not a state adopted an Official English policy in a given year. For the sake of comparability, this study only includes those laws that declare English as the official state language. Other English Only policies aimed specifically at education and voting are not included. For example, California first enacts an English Only voting policy in 1984 and then enacts an Official English law in 1986. In this dataset, California is coded as a zero in 1984 and remains in the dataset until 1986 when the dependent variable becomes a one.

As with the previous analysis, the key independent variable in this analysis measures each state's direct democracy institutions. Two models were estimated: one with a dichotomous indicator of direct democracy institutions and one with the Direct Democracy Impact variable. In this analysis, the measure ranges from zero for non-direct democracy states to 4.997 for California. The average score among direct democracy states is 3.347.

Unlike the previous analysis, it is also necessary to include an interactive term in the model. Similar to the "racial threat" phenomenon in which white voters are more likely to oppose candidates and policies that protect the rights of racial minorities in areas where these minority populations are relatively high, a language-based or ethnic threat has emerged in the literature on U.S. language policy.[38] Tatalovich differentiates between states that have relatively large populations of foreign-language speakers and states that have few foreign-language speakers.[39] As the population of foreign-language speakers in a state grows, the English-speaking majority is expected to feel threatened and more likely to prefer a restrictive language policy. In addition, the foreign language-speaking population also affects the salience of language policy. For states with larger populations of foreign speakers, language policies would have a significant substantive effect on its citizens' lives. For states with small populations of foreign speakers, language policy is more symbolic, less likely to have a significant substantive impact, and consequently less likely to draw opposition.

The policy differences between states with high numbers of foreign-language speakers and states with low numbers have important implications for the effect of direct democracy. As shown by Deborah Schildkraut, direct democracy states should be increasingly likely to pass an Official English law as the number of foreign-language speakers increases.[40] Increased numbers of foreign-language speakers in a state should increase both the substantive impact and relevance of language legislation, but without representative filters in direct democracy states language minorities are put at risk from an increasingly cohesive and salient opinion majority. In states with traditional representative governments, the likelihood of adopting Official English should decrease as the number of foreign-language speakers increases. As language minorities increase in number, their representation in government should also increase, thus decreasing the probability of the states adopting an English Only policy.

To account for this minority threat dynamic, I include a multiplicative term between the direct democracy measures and the percentage of foreign-born residents in each state.[41] The foreign-born population serves as a proxy measure for foreign-language-speakers in each state since data on languages spoken at home are not available for most years of the analysis.[42] If direct democracy does endanger the rights of this minority group, then the slope on the combined effect of the direct democracy variable and the interaction term should increase as the foreign-born population increases. The multiplicative interaction term allows the effect of direct democracy to vary with the level of language threat in a state.

Like the previous section, this analysis also controls for citizen ideology, party control of government, party competition, policy diffusion from neighboring states, population, and education levels. In addition, the models include two new controls, reflecting the different factors that might influence language policy as opposed to marriage recognition policy. Economic hardships, according to conventional wisdom, may lead people to blame immigrants for these problems, and thus increase the propensity for states to adopt anti-immigrant policies.[43] Consequently, states with higher unemployment rates should have a higher likelihood of adopting an Official English law. The final control variable, a dichotomous indicator of whether the state is Southern, accounts for regional differences apparent in the Official English literature.[44] Extending from 1981 to 2007, this study includes an era when the South was considered to be politically exceptional, especially on policies of ethnicity and race. Southern states should be more likely to adopt an Official English law in a given year.

The results from the Cox proportional hazards analyses of the adoption of Official English are shown in Table 2.5. Though the estimates from the model are fairly consistent with the results from the same-sex marriage ban analysis, this evidence is not quite as clear cut. Interpretation requires the consideration of both the interaction coefficient and the original direct democracy coefficient together. When considered alone, the direct democracy coefficient indicates the effect of these institutions when the foreign-born population is zero. Thus, it is not surprising that both direct democracy coefficients are negative when there are essentially no speakers of foreign languages in a state. With a completely homogenous population, there is little need for a language policy, and certainly no threat from a minority group. However, if the population of foreign-born residents is greater than zero, the effect of direct democracy cannot be interpreted solely from the Direct Democracy Impact coefficient. Taken together these

TABLE 2.5 State Adoptions of Official English, 1981–2007

Variable	(1) Coefficient	p-value	(2) Coefficient	p-value
Direct democracy	**−1.581**	**(0.080)**	—	—
Direct Democracy Impact	—	—	**−0.431**	**(0.077)**
Percent foreign born [−]	**−0.435**	**(0.026)**	**−0.423**	**(0.007)**
Direct democracy X foreign born [+]	**0.503**	**(0.016)**	—	—
Direct Democracy Impact X foreign born [+]	—	—	**0.147**	**(0.002)**
Citizen ideology [−]	−0.023	(0.135)	**−0.029**	**(0.089)**
Republican government [+]	0.694	(0.199)	0.859	(0.159)
Democratic government [−]	**−1.058**	**(0.092)**	−1.008	(0.100)
Party competition [+]	−1.138	(0.770)	−0.165	(0.967)
Bordering states w/laws [+]	0.010	(0.498)	0.231	(0.445)
Population (log) [−]	−0.395	(0.124)	**−0.611**	**(0.051)**
Educational attainment [−]	0.117	(0.185)	0.089	(0.319)
Unemployment rate [+]	−0.070	(0.675)	−0.112	(0.526)
Southern state [+]	**3.158**	**(0.002)**	**3.665**	**(0.001)**
Observations	827		827	
Log likelihood	−53.917		−51.725	

Notes: p-values in parentheses (one-tailed tests where appropriate); expected direction of coefficient in brackets; p<0.1 in bold.

coefficients show that states with direct democracy institutions will have an increasing likelihood of adopting an Official English law as the foreign-born population increases. Conversely, states without direct democracy have a decreasing likelihood of adopting this policy as the foreign-born population increases.

This relationship is more apparent when examining the predicted hazard rates of adopting Official English for a given year. It is clear from Figure 2.6 that, as the percentage of foreign-language speakers increases in states with direct democracy, the likelihood of adoption also increases.[45] As seen in the first graph (estimated from Model 1), when the foreign-born population accounts for more than 3 percent of the resident population, the propensity to adopt Official English is significantly higher for direct democracy states compared with non-direct democracy states. The second two graphs show the interaction effects from Model 2. A similar pattern is seen in the second graph, where an average direct democracy state is compared with a non-direct democracy state. Again, when the foreign-born population is above 3 percent the propensity for direct democracy states to adopt the policy is significantly greater. The last graph adds a line for high-impact direct democracy states (with a Direct Democracy Impact score of 5). The change from an average-impact direct democracy state to a high-impact state shows a massive difference, with the propensity of adoption for high-impact states dwarfing the hazard rates for the other two sets of states. This highlights how the arrangements of direct democracy institutions can have a drastic impact on policy outcomes.

Together, these results suggest that, as the number of foreign-born residents in a state increases, the majority should be increasingly threatened and in favor of restrictive language policies like Official English. The positive slopes of the direct democracy lines show an increasing responsiveness to this threatened majority. Anecdotal evidence also supports this finding. Florida Official English activists in 1987 contended that Florida citizens perceived a "threat" in the increasing numbers of Spanish-speaking people in the state.[46] With Official English legislation stalled in the legislature, "threatened" Floridians circumvented their elected officials and passed the language policy on their own with a ballot initiative.

Figure 2.6 also shows an interesting pattern in non-initiative states. While these states have a relatively higher hazard of adopting Official English when the foreign-born population is very low, the hazard rate decreases as the percentages increase. This pattern supports the concept of representative government providing a filter to protect minority rights. As the foreign-born population grows in a state, it should also gain representation in the legislative process. The more representation this minority group has in traditional representative governments, the more the legislative filters should work to protect minority interests and the less likely it is that these governments will adopt anti-minority policies. So despite the increased preference for a restrictive language policy among the English-speaking majority, language minorities are better able to oppose Official English legislation

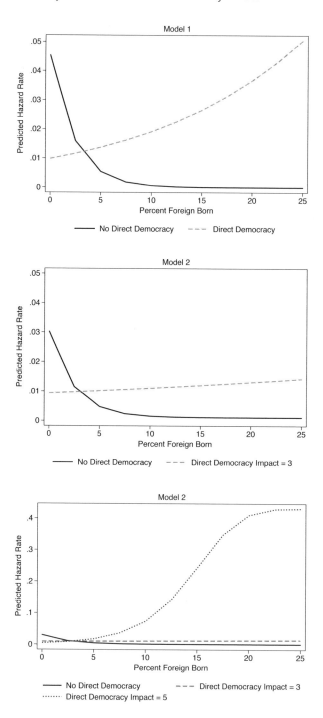

FIGURE 2.6 Hazard Rates of Adopting Official English, 1994

as their numbers grow. This result is consistent with Sean Nicholson-Crotty's findings that diversity moderates the effectiveness of representative institutions in protecting minority rights.[47]

Though the direct democracy and foreign-born variables seem to drive the models, a few other variables show marginally significant effects. Ideologically more liberal states, larger states, and states with Democratic Party governments are less likely to pass Official English laws. Finally, there is a large and significant difference between Southern states and other states.

Overall, the evidence here supports the "tyranny of the majority" argument in the case of Official English. While the effect of direct democracy is moderated by the foreign-born population in a state, these institutions nonetheless increase the probability of adopting this anti-minority policy. When the issue is made sufficiently salient and the majority English-speaking population is united by the threat of increasing numbers of foreign speakers, direct democracy facilitates the adoption of Official English. As with the spread of same-sex marriage bans, citizen legislation only directly led to policy adoption in six states. However, when the indirect effect of citizen legislation is also accounted for, it is clear that direct democracy states have a higher propensity of adopting Official English than do non-direct democracy states.

Affirmative Action Bans

So far, this chapter has shown evidence that direct democracy institutions have played significant roles in the adoption of two contemporary anti-minority policies that have diffused across many American states. In this section I examine one final anti-minority policy: affirmative action bans. This policy area presents some interesting differences from the other two policies that should help to further test the "tyranny of the majority" argument. Unlike same-sex marriage bans and Official English, policies banning or severely limiting affirmative action have only been adopted in a small number of states.

Another difference is more substantive. While the previous two policies clearly restrict the rights of minority groups relative to the majority group, affirmative action bans arguably could be described as rolling back minority rights to be equal to the rights of the majority group. Due to this difference, it is not surprising that proponents of affirmative action bans have taken up the language of civil rights and equality.[48] Still, in banning affirmative action plans, states are effectively adopting policies that specifically target minority groups by restricting the opportunities that these minority groups have for employment, advancement, and education. Affirmative action programs were not implemented to grant equal rights, but rather to provide equal opportunities to groups that have been historically discriminated against. Advocates of these programs contend that dismantling them would leave minority groups without equal opportunities in these areas. Thus, this issue can be considered as a policy that effectively restricts the rights of minority groups and is one that has been studied in terms of the impact of direct democracy institutions.[49] So if direct democracy does endanger minority rights, then it should also apply to this case where a united majority is targeting the (arguably enhanced) rights of minorities.

Affirmative action policies have long been the center of heated debates, but it is only recently that these policies have been targeted by statutory bans. Affirmative action policies were initially developed in the 1960s as a way to remedy or "level the playing field" in education and employment after decades of segregation and discrimination.[50] Using Title VII of the Civil Rights Act and several executive orders, the Johnson and Nixon administrations utilized policies of affirmative action to remove barriers to equality for minorities. The 1970s saw affirmative action policies extended from government employment to private employment and education. The minorities under these affirmative action policies included African Americans, Hispanics, other ethnic minorities, and women.

Throughout this period, opponents of affirmative action contended that these policies violated nondiscrimination laws and were essentially government-sanctioned "reverse discrimination." The backlash to affirmative action was initially rebutted by the courts in several decisions (e.g., *University of California v. Allan Bakke*) in the 1970s, but found new support in the 1980s. The Reagan Administration gave a national voice to opponents of affirmative action and through conservative court appointments was able to effectively whittle away at the scope of these programs over the next fifteen years.

By the mid-1990s, the debate spread from the courts to state legislatures and governors, which began considering statutory action to eliminate affirmative action policies. In California, Governor Pete Wilson began to dismantle the state's affirmative action policies with an executive order in 1995. That same year, Regent Ward Connerly—a Wilson appointee—led a movement within the University of California (UC) Regents to end affirmative action. With two votes, the Board of Regents eliminated preferences for minorities and women in UC employment and admissions. The next year, Connerly and Californians Against Discrimination and Preferences (CADAP) led a campaign to pass Proposition 209, a ballot initiative that would ban affirmative action by the government "in the operation of public employment, public education, or public contracting." The initiative passed with 54 percent of the vote. Soon after, Connerly helped found the American Civil Rights Institute (ACRI) to continue the anti–affirmative action movement across the nation.

Since 1996, eight states have adopted bans on affirmative action (see Table 2.6). Five of the states have enacted far-reaching bans that affect employment, education, and public contracting. The others have more narrow policies, applying only to police and fire department hiring or public employment. In terms of direct democracy's direct impact in this policy area, four of the states used citizen legislation to enact their bans. Each of these policies was comprehensive in scope. Furthermore, every state that has adopted an affirmative action ban has direct

TABLE 2.6 States with Affirmative Action Bans

State	Year	Type of Adoption	Programs	Direct Democracy Impact
California	1996	Initiative	Employment, education, contracts	5.198
Washington	1998	Initiative	Employment, education, contracts	3.768
Colorado	1999	Legislation	Employment	4.540
Missouri	1999	Legislation	Police and fire employment	2.966
Florida	2000	Executive order	Employment, education, contracts	2.929
Utah	2003	Legislation	Employment	2.907
Michigan	2006	Initiative	Employment, education, contracts	3.823
Nebraska	2008	Initiative	Employment, education, contracts	2.679

democracy institutions and a high Direct Democracy Impact score. Conversely, there is not a single non-initiative state that has adopted an affirmative action ban. With only direct democracy states adopting affirmative action bans, it appears that the "tyranny of the majority" argument is once again supported in this policy area.

Analyses

Event history analysis provides further support this conclusion. Table 2.7 shows the results of a Cox proportional hazards model. The dependent variable is an indicator of whether a state passed an affirmative action ban in a given year and direct democracy is measured using the Direct Democracy Impact scores. Since only direct democracy states have adopted these policies, a model using the simple indicator of direct democracy institutions cannot be estimated because not having these institutions perfectly predicts a non-event. The control variables are similar to the previous analyses, with the addition of a measure of racial diversity.[51] With a statistically significant, positive coefficient, the results show that direct democracy states are more likely to adopt an affirmative action ban than other states. Compared to a non-direct democracy state, an average direct democracy state's odds of adopting this type of policy is more than twelve times higher.

While this result is striking, it should be considered with caution. Since the dataset only includes eight adoptions out of a possible 588 observations, there is the potential for biased estimates. In addition, this analysis treats all the affirmative action bans as equivalent events, even though the scope of the policies varies quite a bit. Thus, it is helpful to take a closer look at the political context surrounding the adoptions of these anti-minority policies.

TABLE 2.7 State Adoptions of Affirmative Action Bans, 1996–2008

Variable	Coefficient	P-value
Direct Democracy Impact [+]	**1.438**	**(0.002)**
Citizen ideology [–]	**−0.124**	**(0.012)**
Republican government [+]	−0.882	(0.561)
Democratic government [–]	1.108	(0.453)
Party competition [+]	0.455	(0.948)
Bordering states w/laws [+]	**−8.309**	**(0.070)**
Racial diversity [–]	−6.907	(0.178)
Population (log) [–]	**1.639**	**(0.043)**
Educational attainment [–]	0.167	(0.115)
Observations	**588**	
Log likelihood	**−14.107**	

Note: p-values in parentheses (one-tailed tests where appropriate); Expected direction of coefficient in brackets; p<0.1 in bold

Of the eight states with affirmative action bans, five are far-reaching, affecting university admissions policies, public employment policies, and public contracting policies. For four of these states—California, Washington, Michigan, and Nebraska—the effect of direct democracy is clear. Each of these states used ballot initiatives to adopt their affirmative action bans. Led by Ward Connerly and the ACRI, the ballot measures easily passed with an average of over 57 percent of the vote. Despite having fairly diverse populations in most of these states, a united majority was able to circumvent the filters of representative government and restrict the rights of minorities in their state.[52] In California, 75 percent of African Americans and Latinos opposed Proposition 209, while two-thirds of white men favored it along with a majority of white women.[53] Similar patterns of support were seen in Washington and Michigan.[54]

The role that direct democracy played in the adoption of a broad affirmative action ban in Florida in 1999 is less obvious. The policy was first issued as an executive order by Governor Jeb Bush (R) on November 9, 1999. The order ended racial preferences in state employment, contracting, and university admissions. It also proposed a "Talented 20 Plan" to ensure admission to the top 20 percent of each high school graduating class as an alternative policy to help maintain diversity. This plan was subsequently approved by the Florida Board of Regents.

Although this policy was enacted unilaterally by the Governor, the political context surrounding its adoption included many actors. Earlier that year, Ward Connerly announced a petition drive to get a proposal similar to California's Proposition 209 and Washington's I-200 on Florida's 2000 ballot. Until 1999, Bush had never advocated a plan to end affirmative action in the state. Indeed, the specter of this type of proposal on the 2000 ballot was not welcomed by the Governor. Bush's brother was running for president that year and Florida was predicted to be an important swing state. The 2000 ballot also include a race for an open U.S. Senate seat. The Republican Party worried that a proposal to ban affirmative action could stimulate African Americans to turn out in massive numbers, thus threatening GOP chances. At the same time, Bush had built his own electoral success in part on a strategy of *rapprochement* with minority and civil rights leaders, and had opposed Connerly's efforts.[55]

More pressure was applied to Bush in early November when newspapers reported that Florida voters supported Connerly's proposal by a margin of more than two to one. With simultaneous pressures to remove the issue from the 2000 election from the GOP, end affirmative action from the public, and support affirmative action from his own electoral coalition, Bush acted unilaterally to impose a moderated anti-affirmative action policy. While his Florida One plan ended racial preferences in employment and contracting, it also called on department leaders to voluntarily take diversity into account in their hiring and contracting processes. It also ended racial preferences in university admissions, but used a percentage plan to adjust for the changes in the policy.

After examining the political context surrounding Bush's executive order, it is clear that direct democracy played a role in the adoption of an affirmative action plan. Connerly's petition drive not only pushed the Governor to address the issue, but with the strong support for the proposal (indicating a united majority) it also pushed him to take action. Normally, the indirect effect of direct democracy is thought of as a pressure on legislators. However, this case shows that the threat of citizen legislation can also put pressure on an elected executive to enact a policy in line with the preferences of the majority at the expense of minority groups.

In all five states that have enacted far-reaching affirmative action bans, direct democracy has played a prominent role in the adoption process. But these types of policy proposals have not been limited just to direct democracy states. Nearly half of non-initiative states have also had affirmative action bans introduced in their legislatures. Yet, none of these bills has been successful. Taking a closer look at one case, New Jersey, provides a good illustration of why affirmation action ban efforts have not yet succeeded in non-direct democracy states. New Jersey has had more proposals to ban affirmative action programs than any other non-initiative state. Opponents of affirmative action have introduced two bills each session that would ban these types of policies, but, to date, neither bill has been able to get out of committee. These bills' failures are somewhat surprising given the relatively high support they have with the public. The sponsor of the bill, Rep. Michael Patrick Carroll (R), notes that, "60 percent to 70 percent of the public supports the idea."

The failures are also surprising in this case, given the high amount of publicity the issue of affirmative action has received in the state in the wake of the *Taxman v. Piscataway Board of Education* case (1996). In 1989, the Piscataway, New Jersey school board was cutting personnel and fired Sharon Taxman, a white teacher, instead of a black teacher. Both were hired on the exact same day and received equal evaluations. The board cited a policy of maintaining diversity in letting Taxman go. She sued the school board, claiming reverse discrimination under title VII of the Civil Rights Act. The case worked its way through the courts and made headlines in 1996 when a federal appeals court ruled that the harm imposed to the non-minority by the loss of their job was greater than the benefit of increased diversity.[56] Over the course of the suit, the *Taxman* case drew both statewide and national attention. Both the Bush administration and the Clinton administration weighed in (on opposite sides) along with other national leaders.[57] The case brought the issue of affirmative action to the gubernatorial race and to several legislative races.

Despite all this attention and the high public support to end these programs in the state, the bills continue to die in committee. If New Jersey is a case where representative democracy is providing a filter to protect minority interests, then we should expect the state to be fairly diverse, with some sort of descriptive representation in the legislature. In terms of population diversity, New Jersey ranks eleventh in the country. In 2000, the state's population was 13.6 percent black, 13.3 percent Hispanic, 5.7 percent Asian, and 72.1 percent white. The legislature, though not completely mirroring the population's diversity, does provide some descriptive representation. According to the National Conference of State Legislatures, the state legislature in 2003 was 13 percent black and 6 percent Hispanic.[58] With this amount of diversity both in the population and in the legislature, minorities are able to filter out policy proposals that would restrict their rights. Even in a climate of heightened attention to affirmative action issues and majority support to end these programs, minority groups have been able to successfully defend their interests in the state government.

Even though the diffusion of affirmative action bans has yet to spread beyond a handful of states, the influence of direct democracy in this process is clear. Ballot initiatives were used directly to enact four of the five most expansive affirmative action bans. In the fifth state, the threat of direct democracy influenced the governor to take unilateral action to enact a more moderate version of the policy. States without direct democracy institutions, meanwhile, have yet to adopt a single affirmative action ban.

Discussion

The analyses in this chapter all consistently produced evidence supporting the thesis that direct democracy endangers minority rights. For each policy, the question was posed, "Given that states had not yet adopted the policy, are direct democracy states more likely to adopt the policy in that year than states without direct democracy institutions?" The results of these analyses all answered this question with a resounding, "yes." Whether it's a same-sex marriage ban, an Official English law, or an affirmative action ban, states with direct democracy institutions are more likely than other states to adopt these anti-minority policies.

While there may be moderating circumstances that affect the public attitudes on a particular issue, as was the case for Official English, citizen legislation consistently increases the ability of a united majority to enact policies that target minority rights. This effect seems to be constant across minority group types, from race to ethnicity to sexual preference. The important factor is the unity of the majority group in its preferences to restrict the rights of minorities in some way.

In addition to the consistent support for the main hypothesis, these analyses also revealed some important findings about the nature of the impact of direct democracy on minority-related policies. By examining both the direct outcomes of citizen legislation as well as the traditional legislative outcomes in initiative states, the indirect effect of direct democracy was readily apparent. In only considering the direct outcomes of citizen legislation, it appeared that direct democracy did not play a significant role in the diffusion of same-sex marriage bans and Official English. At best, this more superficial examination produced mixed results. However, once the indirect effects of direct democracy were accounted for (by including the outcomes of traditional legislation in the analysis), the full influence of direct democracy is readily apparent.

Last, using the Direct Democracy Impact measure presented some interesting implications for how citizen legislative institutions can affect policy outcomes. Clearly, not all direct democracy institutions are the same. The variation in institutional arrangements affects the policy decisions these states produce. In general, states with direct initiatives, less insulated legislatures, easier qualification requirements, and relatively high initiative use were more likely to adopt these anti-minority policies.

3

A REPRESENTATIONAL FILTER?

The Passage of Anti-Minority Policy Proposals

The evidence presented in the previous chapter suggests that states with direct democracy institutions are more likely to adopt specific anti-minority policies in a given year than states without direct democracy institutions. As argued in Chapter 1, the source of the increased propensity for direct democracy states to adopt anti-minority proposals lies in the institutional arrangement that allows citizens to circumvent the filtering processes of representative democracy. Thus, direct democracy states are less likely to reject anti-minority policy proposals than states without direct democracy institutions because these proposals are not subject to the legislative filters of the traditional representational process. In the analyses of same-sex marriage bans, Official English laws, and affirmative action bans it is clear that direct democracy states were more likely to adopt these three policies, but it is still unclear whether this increased propensity to adopt anti-minority policies is a direct consequence of the varying filtering mechanisms of the two institutional arrangements.

In using policy adoption as the unit of analysis, I am not able to examine failed anti-minority policy proposals. If a state does not adopt the policy in a given year, it is coded as a zero, whether or not the policy was even considered. From this perspective, states that reject anti-minority proposals are the same as states that don't even consider them. Similarly, a state that passes one anti-minority proposal out of twenty introduced is equivalent to a state that passes the only anti-minority policy proposal it considers. Again, while event history analysis does provide clear evidence of a state's propensity to adopt a specific policy, it cannot directly verify the underlying foundation of the "tyranny of the majority" argument because it does not explicitly examine whether the filtering mechanisms are actually functioning to protect minority rights. Thus, in order to more directly study this question, it is necessary to consider individual policy proposals.

The "tyranny of the majority" argument implies that an anti-minority policy proposal is more likely to pass in a state with direct democracy institutions because it can avoid or undermine the filtering processes of representative democracy. It follows from this argument that states with direct democracy institutions should have higher rates of passage for anti-minority proposals. In this chapter I examine these implications through an analysis of anti-minority policy proposals considered in the U.S. states over a decade, from 1995 to 2004.

Anti-Minority Policy Proposals

In this study, I examine policies that directly and explicitly restrict the rights of political minorities, and not the broader set of policies that impact the interests of minorities. Again, it is the explicitly anti-minority policies that should be most affected by the majoritarian effects of direct democracy. And, it is these types of issues that most directly affect the rights of minority groups. From 1995 to 2004, there were three minority groups whose rights were commonly targeted by legislation in the American states: homosexuals, Limited English Proficient (LEP) speakers, and minorities in general (by restricting or banning affirmative action programs). These three types of anti-minority proposals were introduced in most states during this ten-year time period. Every state considered at least one anti-homosexual policy. Thirty-four states considered an anti-foreign-language policy, and thirty-one states considered at least one general anti-affirmative action policy. Together, these three policy categories encompass the vast majority of all the anti-minority policies considered during this time period.

While a very limited number of other anti-minority policies were introduced during this period, they tended to be less generalizable to other states and more idiosyncratic in nature. For example, the Arkansas Senate considered a bill in 2003 to limit parking for people with disabilities. Admittedly, by focusing on these three categories, I do not include every single anti-minority policy proposed in the American states over this time period. However, I do examine the most salient and visible minority rights issues of the period: same-sex marriage bans, Official English laws, and affirmative action bans. In addition to being highly relevant, each of the issues covered here bear directly on the fundamental rights of minority groups: the right to marry, raise a family, vote, get an education, get a job, and have equal protection under the law. Again, most anti-minority policies introduced from 1995 to 2004 do fit into one of these three categories and are covered in this analysis.

To identify these anti-minority policy proposals, I conducted keyword searches of the text of all legislative bills and the text of all ballot measures introduced from 1995 to 2004.[1] Table 3.1 shows the types of policy proposals identified in the search by the target group. The most common policy proposals targeting homosexuals were same-sex marriage bans, while the most common policy

TABLE 3.1 Anti-Minority Proposals by Targeted Group, 1995–2004

Homosexuals	LEP speakers	Minorities
Same-sex marriage ban★	Official English★	General affirmative action ban★
Bar homosexuals from adoption and/or foster care	English Only education★	Ban on affirmative action for educational institutions
Ban on benefits for same-sex couples	English Only ballots	Ban on affirmative action for public hiring and contracting
Ban on education of homosexuality	English proficiency requirement for public assistance	Ban on group-norming test scores for employment or admissions
Ban on recognition of civil unions	English Only driver's license exams	Affirmative action restrictions
Ban on sodomy★		

Notes: Proposals in *italics* indicate the most common policy proposal for each target group.

★ Includes constitutional amendments.

TABLE 3.2 Passage Rates of Anti-Minority Proposals by Targeted Group, 1995–2004

	Homosexuals	Foreign speakers	Minorities	All groups
Proposals	335	148	117	600
Passed	64	13	5	82
Percent Passed	19.1	8.78	4.27	13.67

proposals targeting foreign-language speakers and minorities were Official English laws and general affirmative action bans, respectively.

In total, the search yielded 600 proposals (see Table 3.2). Of these, 335 targeted homosexuals, 148 targeted LEP speakers, and 117 targeted minorities in general. Of these 600 proposals, eighty-two passed. The passage rate varied across the targeted groups, with anti-homosexual proposals passing 19 percent of the time and proposals targeting minority groups in general passing about 4 percent of the time.

Direct Democracy vs. Representative Democracy

With the anti-minority proposals identified, I can compare the passage rates between states with direct democracy institutions and states without direct democracy institutions. If direct democracy does reduce the effectiveness of representational filters and endangers minority rights, then anti-minority policy proposals in direct democracy states should pass at a higher rate than non-direct democracy states. In addition to this simple comparison, I also utilize the three measures of direct democracy employed in the principle components analysis from the previous chapter: the Legislative Insulation Index, the Qualification Difficulty Index, and the initiative use count.

Table 3.3 shows the passage rates of these proposals over the various measures of direct democracy discussed above. The first section compares states with direct democracy to those without direct democracy. In the direct democracy states, fifty-three of the 270 considered proposals passed, a rate of nearly 20 percent. States without direct democracy, meanwhile, only passed twenty-nine of 330 proposals—less than half the rate of the states with direct democracy. The last column in the table shows that the difference between the two, at almost 11 percent, is statistically significant.[2]

The last three sections of the table employ the more nuanced measures of direct democracy. Given the small number of states within each scale score, I combine the higher scores into one category, the lower scores into another category, and the non-direct democracy states into another. Using alternative cut points for these categories (e.g., means and median scores of direct democracy states) does not significantly alter the results of the difference of proportions tests employed here. Looking at the legislative insulation categories, there is a marginally significant difference between states with less insulated legislatures and the states with more insulated legislatures: just under 23 percent compared with 16 percent. The difference between states without direct democracy and direct democracy states with relatively more insulated legislatures is also significant, with anti-minority proposals passing at almost twice the rate of the former category. Using the Qualification Difficulty Index produces similar results, but the difference between the two categories of direct democracy is not statistically significant. Still, the primary difference of interest, between direct democracy states and non-direct democracy states, remains robust. The percentage of anti-minority proposals passed in states with relatively difficult qualification requirements more than doubles the percentage passed in states without direct democracy institutions. Comparing passage rates by the states' initiative use over the time period reveals a significant difference between states that use initiatives and states that do not. As with the qualification difficulty comparison, there is no significant difference between high-use states and lower-use states.

No matter how direct democracy is measured, the comparisons show that states with direct democracy institutions pass significantly higher percentages of anti-minority proposals than states without direct democracy institutions. However, since the anti-minority proposals in this study include three types of targeted minority groups, it is also prudent to examine whether this result is robust across the three minority groups. In other words, does the discrepancy in passage rates of anti-minority proposals hold across the different targeted minority groups?

TABLE 3.3 Passage Rates of Anti-Minority Proposals, 1995–2004

	States	Number	Passed	Rate (%)	Difference (%)
By direct democracy					
Direct democracy states	24	270	53	19.63	10.84★★
No direct democracy	26	330	29	8.79	
By legislative insulation					
Least insulated (5–9)	15	145	33	22.76	6.76#
More insulated (1–4)	9	125	20	16.00	
					7.21★
No direct democracy (0)	26	330	29	8.79	
By qualification difficulty					
Least difficulty (5–7)	9	91	19	20.88	1.88
More difficult (1–4)	15	179	34	19.00	
					10.21★★
No direct democracy (0)	26	330	29	8.79	
By initiative use					
High use (>10)	14	154	30	19.48	0.73
Low use (1–10)	9	112	21	18.75	
					9.47★★
No use (0)	27	334	31	9.28	

Notes: Variable score in parentheses.

★★$p<0.01$; ★$p<0.05$; #$p<0.1$.

I address this question by comparing the passage rates of anti-minority proposals in direct democracy states to the passage rates of similar proposals in states without direct democracy across the three types of targeted groups. The results of these comparisons are shown in Table 3.4. The table also examines the difference between states with direct initiatives and those without direct initiatives. For proposals that target homosexuals, a relatively large difference between the states is evident. Likewise, a significantly higher percentage of proposals that target minority groups through affirmative action restrictions pass in states with direct democracy institutions than in non-direct democracy states.

Interestingly, these differences diminish for proposals that target LEP speakers. This may be caused by the minority-threat dynamic discussed in the previous chapter. As the literature on language policy in the American states suggests, when there are relatively low numbers of foreign-speaking individuals in a state, language policy is not a publicly salient issue.[3] However, as the population of foreign speakers increases, the issue of language becomes more salient and the majority may feel threatened. The event history analysis of Official English laws

TABLE 3.4 Anti-Minority Proposal Passage by Targeted Group, 1995–2004

	Proposals	*Passage rate (%)*	*Difference (%)*
Homosexuals			
Direct democracy	153	26.15	12.96
No direct democracy	182	13.19	(0.001)
LEP speakers			
Direct democracy	61	13.11	7.37
No direct democracy	87	5.75	(0.060)
Minorities			
Direct democracy	56	8.93	8.93
No direct democracy	61	0.00	(0.009)

Note: *p*-values for one-tailed tests in parentheses.

shows that, among states with large foreign-born populations, direct democracy states are more likely to adopt these policies than states without direct democracy. This interactive effect between direct democracy and the size of the foreign-speaking population on the likelihood of adopting Official English should also extend to the passage rates of proposals that target foreign speakers.

To test this expectation, I grouped the states by their foreign-born population and compared passage rate of anti-LEP speaker proposals (see Table 3.5). In states with low populations of foreign-born individuals, there is no difference in the percentage of proposals that pass. In the states with higher levels of foreign-born individuals, however, the difference between direct democracy states and states without direct democracy is quite large and statistically significant. Although the dichotomy of low and high foreign-born populations is a blunt way to assess this interactive effect, the results do support the idea that threat or public salience affect the impact that direct democracy has on language policies and mirrors the results from the previous chapter.

One final way to compare direct democracy states with non-direct democracy states is to examine the average percentage of anti-minority proposals that each state passes. Table 3.6 shows the passage rates for each state over this time period. The states in the left column are the states with direct democracy institutions. The averages for each type of state are presented in the bottom rows. These comparisons show an even starker difference between the states. On average, direct democracy states pass more than 30 percent of their anti-minority proposals, over 20 percentage points more than states without direct democracy. Comparing the nineteen states with direct initiatives to other states, the gap grows even larger. Direct initiative states pass the proposals at a rate of over 36 percent while non-direct initiative states have a passage rate of just less than 14 percent.

TABLE 3.5 Passage Rates of Proposals Targeting Foreign Speakers, 1995–2004

	Proposals	Passage rate (%)	Difference (%)
Foreign-born population ≤5% (19 states)			
Direct democracy	32	9.38	0.86
No direct democracy	47	8.51	(0.447)
Foreign-born population >5% (18 states)			
Direct democracy	40	17.86	15.36
No direct democracy	28	2.50	(0.014)

Note: p-values for one-tailed tests in parentheses.

TABLE 3.6 Passage Rates of Anti-Minority Proposals by State, 1995–2004

Direct democracy states			Non-direct democracy states		
State	Proposals	Passage rate (%)	State	Proposals	Passage rate (%)
Alaska	5	60.00	Alabama	28	3.57
Arizona	7	28.57	Connecticut	4	0.00
Arkansas	5	60.00	Delaware	5	20.00
California	17	17.65	Georgia	14	28.57
Colorado	18	11.11	Hawaii	21	4.76
Florida	2	50.00	Indiana	7	14.29
Idaho	3	33.33	Iowa	17	11.76
Illinois	3	33.33	Kansas	9	11.11
Maine	5	20.00	Kentucky	10	20.00
Massachusetts	11	9.09	Louisiana	11	18.18
Michigan	20	15.00	Maryland	8	0.00
Mississippi	35	5.71	Minnesota	16	6.25
Missouri	43	13.95	New Hampshire	7	14.29
Montana	5	60.00	New Jersey	25	0.00
Nebraska	5	20.00	New Mexico	10	0.00
Nevada	3	66.67	New York	29	0.00
North Dakota	2	100.00	North Carolina	7	14.29
Ohio	12	16.67	Pennsylvania	15	6.67
Oklahoma	24	12.50	Rhode Island	2	0.00
Oregon	10	10.00	South Carolina	22	4.55
South Dakota	4	50.00	Tennessee	4	25.00
Utah	6	83.33	Texas	14	7.14
Washington	21	9.52	Vermont	10	10.00
Wyoming	4	25.00	Virginia	6	66.67
			West Virginia	19	5.26
			Wisconsin	10	10.00
Average	11.25	33.81**	Average	12.69	11.63**

Note: **significantly different at the 0.01 level from the corresponding average percent in the same row.

Table 3.6 also reveals that direct democracy states, on average, consider roughly equal numbers of anti-minority proposals as non-direct democracy states. If anything, states without direct democracy consider more anti-minority proposals than direct democracy states. Direct democracy states averaged just over eleven anti-minority proposals during this time period, while non-direct democracy states considered over twelve anti-minority proposals, on average. This is important because it underscores the point that direct democracy states are not adopting anti-minority policies because they are more exposed to these types of proposals. Rather, direct democracy states are proposing slightly fewer anti-minority proposals, but passing them at a significantly higher rate. Direct democracy states do not seem to be more likely to consider anti-minority proposals; they are just more likely to pass them given the ability of the citizens to circumvent the filtering mechanisms of representative government. In contrast, though non-direct democracy states are considering roughly the same number of anti-minority policy proposals, they pass these policies at a significantly lower rate. This strongly suggests that the representational filters are functioning to protect minority rights in these states.

In all, the descriptive data tend to support the findings from the previous chapter. In comparing the passage rates of anti-minority policy proposals, direct democracy states pass higher percentages of proposals they considered than states without direct democracy. This relationship holds across varying indicators of direct democracy and across the three targeted minority groups.

Direct Democracy and Anti-Minority Proposal Passage

While cross-tabulation comparisons certainly provide support for the anti-minority impact of direct democracy and for the protective filtering mechanisms of representative democracy, it cannot account for other determinants of anti-minority proposal passage, like public ideology and party control of the government. Obviously, there are a myriad of factors that can influence whether a single policy proposal is ultimately adopted by the state. In order to assess the effect of direct democracy while also controlling for other possible determinants of anti-minority proposal passage, I estimate two logistic regression models where the unit of analysis is each individual proposal. This approach asks the following question: For any given anti-minority proposal, is it more likely to pass in a direct democracy state or a state without direct democracy?

The dependent variable is a simple indicator of whether or not an anti-minority policy proposal was passed. It does not distinguish between ballot measures and legislative bills since the study is trying to gauge the total effect of direct democracy, not just the direct effect. The primary independent variable of inter-est measures a state's direct democracy institutions. As in the previous chapter, an index of Direct Democracy Impact is generated from a principle components analysis of the Legislative Insulation Index, the Qualification Difficulty Index, and the use of initiatives in the state over the time period in question. As with the previous analyses I expect a positive coefficient on this variable, indicating that direct democracy states are more likely to adopt anti-minority proposals than states without direct democracy.

The other possible determinants of anti-minority proposal passage can be grouped into three general categories: government attributes, state attributes, and proposal attributes. The government attributes include party variables and measures of the institutional attributes of the legislature. To account for party effects, three variables are employed. Party control of the state government is measured with two dichotomous indicators of whether the Republican or Democratic Party has control of the legislature and the governorship. The base category in these models is divided government. I expect Republican governments to be more likely to pass anti-minority proposals and Democratic governments to be less likely to pass these proposals. The folded Ranney Index is also included to account for party competition.[4] The models also account for institutional aspects of the state legislatures, including legislative professionalization, the size of the legislature, and whether or not one of the chambers has a limit on the number of bills that can be introduced.[5] Larger and more professional legislatures tend to consider more bills in each session and thus should be less likely to pass any single bill. Conversely, legislatures with bill introduction limits should be more likely to pass a bill.

In addition to governmental attributes, the models also control for several state attributes. First, citizen ideology is taken into account using the Berry, Ringquist, Fording, and Hanson measure.[6] More liberal states should be less likely to pass anti-minority proposals. Minority diversity is also accounted for using Hero's diversity measure.[7] More diverse states should be less likely to pass anti-minority proposals. Several other demographic characteristics of the states are also included in the model: educational attainment (percent of population with a college degree), unemployment rate, and population (logged). States with more educated populations should be more tolerant, and thus should be less likely to pass an anti-minority proposal.[8] Economic bad times may increase anti-minority sentiment and thus increase the likelihood of passage.[9] Finally, following arguments from *The Federalist Papers*, larger states should be better able to overcome the problems of majority factions and thus less likely to pass anti-minority proposals.[10]

The last group of control variables account for the attributes of the anti-minority proposals themselves.[11] Constitutional amendments often require supermajorities for approval, and should be less likely to pass than proposals that can pass with a simple majority. Thus, the models include the proportion of votes required to pass (0.5, 0.6, 0.67, or 0.75). Proposals that are competing for passage with several other similar proposals should also be less likely to pass. Finally, I control for the minority group that is being targeted by the proposal. In the last decade, many more anti-homosexual policies have been adopted than other anti-minority proposals. Thus, proposals that target homosexuals should be the most likely to pass. Since only a few states have adopted anti-affirmative action policies, these proposals should be least likely to pass of the three targeted groups.

Results

The results from these models, estimated using a logistic regression with robust standard errors clustered on the state, are presented in Table 3.7. Given the binary nature of the dependent variable and the relatively low percentage of proposals that passed, both models fit relatively well, and are certainly improvements over the null prediction.[12]

TABLE 3.7 Determinants of the Passage of Anti-Minority Bills, 1995–2004

Variable	(1)		(2)	
	Coefficient	p-value	Coefficient	p-value
Direct democracy [+]	**0.874**	**(0.002)**	—	—
Direct Democracy Impact [+]	—	—	**0.291**	**(0.002)**
Government attributes				
Republican control [+]	**0.856**	**(0.017)**	**0.919**	**(0.010)**
Democratic control [–]	–0.035	(0.458)	–0.009	(0.489)
Party competition [–]	0.099	(0.485)	–0.146	(0.478)
Professionalization [–]	–1.405	(0.223)	–1.377	(0.227)
Size of legislature [–]	0.001	(0.374)	0.002	(0.525)
Introduction limits [+]	**0.693**	**(0.053)**	**0.578**	**(0.076)**
State attributes				
Citizen ideology [–]	–0.004	(0.393)	–0.007	(0.306)
Minority diversity [–]	0.120	(0.465)	0.571	(0.661)
Educational attainment [–]	–0.033	(0.241)	–0.045	(0.184)
Unemployment [+]	–0.169	(0.212)	–0.177	(0.198)
Population (logged) [–]	–0.073	(0.402)	–0.176	(0.279)
Proposal attributes				
Supermajority required [–]	–3.185	(0.150)	–3.139	(0.151)
Similar bills in session [–]	**–0.406**	**(0.001)**	**–0.370**	**(0.002)**
Targets homosexuals [+]	**1.976**	**(0.000)**	**2.018**	**(0.000)**
Targets foreign speakers [+]	**1.047**	**(0.033)**	**1.114**	**(0.030)**
Constant	0.269	(0.938)	1.302	(0.694)
Observations	595		595	
Log pseudolikelihood	–193.333		–192.520	
McKelvey & Zavoina R^2	0.322		0.330	

Notes: p-values in parentheses (one-tailed tests where appropriate); expected direction of coefficient in brackets; p<0.1 in bold.

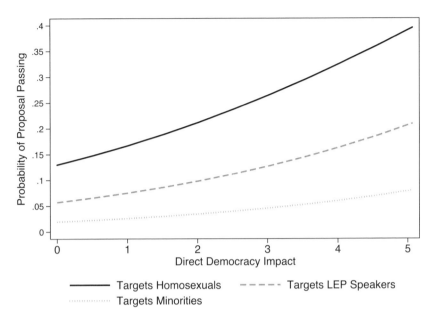

FIGURE 3.1 Predicted Probabilities of an Anti-Minority Proposal Passing

As expected, both direct democracy coefficients are positive and significant, providing further support to the findings from the previous analyses. The first model shows that anti-homosexual proposals in direct democracy states are significantly more likely to pass than in other states. Holding all variables at their mean or modal values, the probability of an anti-gay proposal passing nearly doubles from 14.5 percent in non-direct democracy states to 28.8 percent in direct democracy states. The predicted probability of passing proposals targeting LEP speakers rises from 6.3 percent to 13.8 percent. The predicted probability of passing proposals targeting general minorities rises from 2.3 percent to 5.3 percent.

The second model shows that states with high-impact direct democracy institutions are more likely to pass anti-minority proposals than both states without direct democracy and states with relatively low-impact direct democracy institutions. Figure 3.1 shows the magnitude of this effect by targeted group, with predicted probabilities of passing rising significantly as Direct Democracy Impact increases. The results show that there are significant differences in the likelihood of passing anti-minority policies both within direct democracy states and between these states and states without direct democracy institutions.

Though the predicted probabilities from these models never rise above 0.4, a passage rate of 10–30 percent is not very low for legislative passage rates in the American states.[13] The important aspect of these findings is not that anti-minority bills have exceptionally high probabilities of passing in direct democracy states, but rather that they have a significantly higher probability of passing compared with similar bills in non-direct democracy states. In each case, direct democracy states showed significant increases in the probability of passing these proposals compared with other states. And, it is the comparison between the two types of systems that most directly tests the "tyranny of majority" critique.

The models also show some other significant predictors of anti-minority proposal passage. Compared with divided governments and Democratic-controlled governments, Republican Party control increases the likelihood of passing these proposals. Legislatures with bill introduction limits are marginally more likely to pass these anti-minority bills. In addition, the attributes of the proposal have significant impacts on the likelihood of passage. As the number of similar proposals considered in the same session increases, the likelihood that of any one of them passes decreases. There are also significant differences in the likelihood of passing depending on the minority group that is targeted. Proposals that target homosexuals and foreign speakers are more likely to pass than proposals that target minorities in general. The difference between proposals that target homosexuals and proposals that target foreign speakers is also statistically significant.

Discussion

The argument that direct democracy endangers minority rights, as discussed earlier, is a comparison between two institutional arrangements. It is not that citizen legislative institutions necessarily have a negative impact on minority rights, but rather that they are relatively more likely to have this type of policy effect than representative democratic institutions. It follows that the hypothesis that derives from this argument is, itself, comparative as well. Namely, states with direct democracy institutions are more likely to adopt policies that restrict the rights of minority groups than states without direct democracy institutions. The most direct way to test this hypothesis is to compare the outcomes of anti-minority policy proposals in governments with the two types of institutional arrangements.

The results in this study are unambiguous. From 1995 to 2004 states with direct democracy institutions passed anti-minority proposals at a significantly higher rate than states without direct democracy. By extending the analysis to not only examine instances of policy adoption, but also instances of failed policy proposals, it is clear that anti-minority proposals in direct democracy states fared much better than comparable proposals in states without direct democracy. Furthermore, the finding that states with traditional, representative democracies filter out a higher percentage of anti-minority proposals than their direct democracy counterparts extends across the three targeted minority groups under examination here.

By comparing all anti-minority proposals introduced in direct democracy states to the anti-minority proposals introduced in states without direct democracy institutions, the study was also able to account for both the direct and indirect effects of citizen legislation. Where previous research on direct democracy and minority rights tended to focus on the direct outcomes of citizen legislation, this study examined legislative bills that target minority groups in direct democracy states in addition to the proposals considered by voters on the ballot. In doing so, the total impact of direct democracy institutions on the likelihood of an anti-minority policy proposal passing was clear: The presence of direct democracy in a state increases the probability of passing an anti-minority proposal.

4

THE FLIP SIDE

Direct Democracy and Pro-Minority Policies

So far, this study has examined how anti-minority policies fare in states with direct democracy mechanisms as compared with similar policies in states without these institutions. In looking at policies that explicitly restrict the rights of minority groups, the results have been unambiguous: States with direct democracy are more likely to pass anti-minority policies than other states. While these results support the "tyranny of the majority" argument, that the rights of minority groups are endangered under pure democracy systems, they do not tell the entire story of minority rights and direct democracy. Just as states can pass laws that restrict minority rights, they can also adopt policies that protect and enhance the rights of minorities. Although direct democracy states pass anti-minority measures at higher rates than non-direct democracy states, and are more likely to adopt specific anti-minority policies, it is not clear from the previous chapters or from the existing literature how pro-minority policies fare under direct democracy systems.

The very language of pro-minority policies, like nondiscrimination and civil rights, may engender more widespread support for these policies than opposition to anti-minority policies. If this is the case, direct democracy may actually increase the likelihood of passing these types of policies. An important caveat to Madison's concerns about the tyranny of the majority is the extent to which the majority group is unified in purpose against minorities. If pro-minority policy proposals do not unify the majority in opposition, but rather unify them in support, then direct democracy may actually facilitate the adoption of these policies. This could act as a balance to the tyrannical outcomes seen in the previous chapter. Alternatively, the tyrannical effect of direct democracy that was evident in previous chapters may continue to hold for pro-minority policies, which would put the rights of minorities under these systems at further risk. Currently, it is not clear how direct democracy impacts the adoption of pro-minority policies.

Little, if any, work has focused solely on policies that protect or expand the rights of minorities. Existing research on direct democracy and minority rights tends to aggregate both pro- and anti-minority policy proposals together and evaluate the direction of the outcomes.[1] Haider-Markel, Querze, and Lindaman's 2007 study of gay rights legislation did separate the two types of policy proposals and found that pro-gay measures tended to outnumber anti-gay measures in state legislatures, but anti-gay measures outnumbered pro-gay measures on ballot measures.[2] However, in examining the outcomes of these policy proposals, the authors aggregated both types of gay-related legislation. They then evaluated the direction of the outcome (pro- or anti-gay), but did not account for whether the proposal was intended to protect or restrict gay rights. Thus, it remains unclear if direct democracy affects pro-minority measures differently than anti-minority measures.

To evaluate the impact of direct democracy on the adoption of policies that explicitly protect or expand minority rights, I examine four specific pro-minority policies using a similar approach to the analyses in Chapter 2 on anti-minority policies. The first section evaluates the expansion of state nondiscrimination policies to include sexual orientation, which protect gay rights. The next section examines racial profiling bans, which protect several racial and ethnic minorities. The third section undertakes an analysis of hate crime laws, which offer expanded protection to most minority groups. The final section examines a particular set of state hate crime laws—those that include sexual orientation. In each section I evaluate the impact of direct democracy on the adoption of these specific policies by comparing direct democracy states with non-direct democracy states.

Sexual Orientation and Nondiscrimination Laws

One of the most fundamental pro-minority policies a state can pass is a nondis-crimination law. These civil rights policies outlaw discrimination in employment, housing, education, and public accommodations.[3] Every state has some form of a nondiscrimination law. Most states originally barred discriminatory practices based on race, ethnicity, gender, and religion. However, since the late 1980s many states have expanded them to include sexual orientation and gender identity.[4] By 2008, twenty states had laws on the books that outlaw discrimination based on sexual orientation.

The inclusion of sexual orientation in nondiscrimination laws was a focal point in the gay rights movement of the 1970s. The gay rights movement had gained momentum following the Stonewall Riots in 1969, sparking the organization of more than 800 homosexual political groups by 1973.[5] At the national level, congressional supporters sought to expand the 1964 Civil Rights Acts to include sexual orientation, but they were unsuccessful. The movement found more success at the local level. In 1973, East Lansing, Michigan became the first city to ban discriminatory practices against homosexuals. San Francisco followed two months

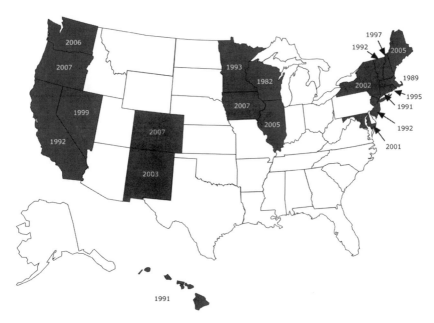

FIGURE 4.1 Adoptions of Non-Discrimination Laws That Include Sexual
Orientation, 1982–2007

later with its own nondiscrimination law. Today, over one hundred local governments include sexual orientation in their nondiscrimination policies. Despite the
adoption of these policies at the local level, however, state and federal lawmakers
continued to resist passing similar laws.

It was not until 1982 that Wisconsin became the first state to pass a nondiscrimination law that extended protection to homosexuals. Seven more years
would pass before another state followed suit. After a backlash against the gay
rights movement in the late 1970s, the debate shifted away from anti-discrimination policy to center on the AIDS epidemic during the 1980s. Though no
state adopted this type of nondiscrimination policy during this period, there was
growing acceptance of gay rights in the United States. By the end of the 1980s,
the focus of the movement shifted back towards anti-discrimination policy. From
1989 to 1999, eight states added sexual orientation to their nondiscrimination
policies. Eight more have passed these policies from 2000 to 2007. Figure 4.1
shows the states that have adopted comprehensive nondiscrimination policies that
include sexual orientation.

The patterns of yearly and cumulative adoptions of these policies at the state
level are presented in Figure 4.2. The flat line through much of the 1980s shows
the reluctance of state policymakers to follow Wisconsin's initial adoption.
However, a more traditional pattern of policy diffusion emerges in the 1990s,
shown by a clear S-shape in the cumulative adoptions from 1989 to 1995. In the

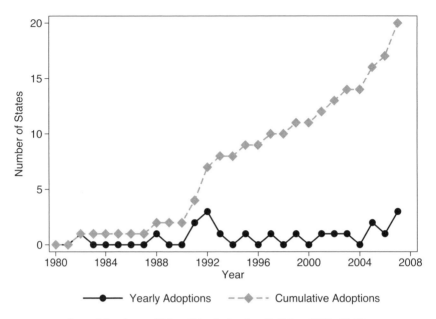

FIGURE 4.2 State Adoptions of Non-Discrimination Policies, 1982–2007

late 1990s the adoption rate slowed to one state every other year, but the more recent increase in the cumulative line suggests a new burst of policy adoption.

From Figures 4.1 and 4.2, it is clear that the spread of policies to protect homosexuals from discrimination has been relatively incremental since 1980. Nonetheless, 40 percent of the states have adopted these policies during this time period. So what role, if any, has direct democracy played in the diffusion of pro-minority policies?

In terms of a direct effect of direct democracy institutions, only six ballot measures addressing the inclusion of sexual orientation in nondiscrimination policies have been considered since 1970 (shown in Table 4.1). Five of these measures sought to restrict the rights of homosexuals by explicitly banning the inclusion of sexual orientation in the state's nondiscrimination policies or by vetoing a policy passed by the government. The only two ballot measures to add sexual orientation to the state's nondiscrimination law—Oregon's 1988 ballot initiative and Maine's 2000 legislative referendum—were both defeated handily. The only pro-minority outcome was the failed popular veto of Maine's nondiscrimination policy in 2005. This was the third time the Maine government had passed this policy, but the previous popular veto attempt in 1998 was successful and a subsequent legislative referendum in 2000 failed to win majority support. Thus, for state nondiscrimination policies, it seems that the only direct effect of direct democracy may be to inhibit their passage.

TABLE 4.1 Ballot Measures Addressing Sexual Orientation and Nondiscrimination

State	Year	Ballot measure	Outcome
Colorado	1992	*Amendment 2*: Initiative to amend the state Constitution to prohibit the inclusion of sexual orientation in nondiscrimination policies	Passed (53.4%): *anti-minority*
Maine	1998	*Question 1*: Popular referendum to reject a ban on discrimination based on sexual orientation passed by the legislature and signed by the governor	Passed (51.3%): *anti-minority*
Maine	2000	*Question 6*: Legislative referendum to ratify a nondiscrimination law including sexual orientation that was passed by the legislature and signed by the governor	Failed (45%): *anti-minority*
Maine	2005	*Question 1*: Popular referendum to reject a ban on discrimination based on sexual orientation passed by the legislature and signed by the governor	Failed (45%): *pro-minority*
Oregon	1988	*Measure 8*: Initiative to revoke a ban on sexual orientation discrimination in the state executive branch	Passed (52.8%): *anti-minority*
Washington	1997	*Initiative 677*: Prohibits discrimination based on sexual orientation	Failed (40.3%): *anti-minority*

Source: National Conference of State Legislatures.

Beyond just the direct influence of citizen legislation, other evidence also suggests that direct democracy states may be less likely to adopt these laws than non-direct democracy states. Of the twenty states that currently have a nondiscrimination policy that includes sexual orientation, only eight of them are direct democracy states. Only a third of direct democracy states have adopted this policy, compared with 46 percent of non-direct democracy states. While these simple comparisons are far from conclusive, they do support the "tyranny of the majority" argument.

Event History Analyses

To more closely examine the relationship between direct democracy and the adoption of nondiscrimination laws that include sexual orientation, it is necessary to also consider other determinants of policy adoption. As in Chapter 2, event history analysis is utilized to answer the following question: Given that a state has not adopted a nondiscrimination policy that includes sexual orientation in previous years, what is the probability that it will do so in that year?

Yearly data has been collected on forty-nine states from 1982 to 2008.[6] The analysis begins in 1982 with the first adoption of a state-level nondiscrimination policy that includes sexual orientation by Wisconsin. Since Delaware and Hawaii adopted these policies after 2008, the dataset is clearly right-censored. Due to the nature of the data, a Cox proportion hazards model that uses the exact discrete method for ties is, again, well-suited to address this question. The dependent variable in this analysis is a dichotomous indicator of whether or not a state adopted a nondiscrimination policy that includes sexual orientation in a given year. Once a state adopts its initial policy to protect the rights of homosexuals, it is dropped from the dataset. Thus, states like California, Rhode Island, and New Jersey, who all initially adopted protections based on sexual orientation and later passed protection for gender identity or expression, are not included in the dataset after their initial adoption.

As with the previous analyses, I estimate two models: one model using a dichotomous indicator of direct democracy institutions and one using the Direct Democracy Impact measure. A negative coefficient on these variables would suggest another negative impact on the rights of minorities, while a positive coefficient would suggest that direct democracy may have a positive effect in for this pro-minority policy.

I also control for several other potential determinants of policy adoption.[7] Like the previous chapters in this book, these analyses control for citizen ideology, party control of government, party competition, geographic diffusion from neighboring states, population, and education levels.[8] Given the minority group in question, I also include estimates of the numbers of same-sex households, the evangelical population, and a dichotomous indicator for whether or not that state has a sodomy ban (prior to *Lawrence v. Texas*, 2003).[9]

The results from the Cox proportional hazards analyses of the adoption of nondiscrimination policies that include sexual orientation are shown in Table 4.2. Like the previous analyses, the coefficients can be interpreted in a similar manner to conditional logistic regression coefficients, as the effect of a one unit change in the independent variable has on the odds of a state adopting this type of nondiscrimination policy in a particular year.

As in the previous analyses, the direct democracy coefficients are negative, but in this case they are not statistically significant. From these models, there does not seem to be a difference in the propensity to adopt nondiscrimination policies covering sexual orientation between direct democracy states and states without direct democracy. This may reflect the contrast in the popularity of nondiscrimination policies (and other policies that claim civil rights goals) on one hand and the opposition to gay rights on the other hand.

Looking at the control variables, the adoption of this type of nondiscrimination policy is driven entirely by partisan control of government and education levels in a state. As expected, governments controlled by the Democratic Party are significantly more likely than Republican or divided governments to adopt these

TABLE 4.2 Adoptions of Nondiscrimination Laws Including Sexual Orientation, 1982–2007

	(1)		(2)	
Variable	*Coefficient*	*p-value*	*Coefficient*	*p-value*
Direct democracy [−]	−0.422	(0.231)	—	—
Direct Democracy Impact [−]	—	—	−0.117	(0.243)
Citizen ideology [+]	0.034	(0.106)	0.033	(0.110)
Evangelical rate [−]	−0.008	(0.123)	−0.008	(0.124)
Same-sex households [+]	1.234	(0.230)	1.308	(0.221)
Democratic government [+]	**1.304**	**(0.013)**	**1.276**	**(0.014)**
Party competition [+]	−2.349	(0.268)	−2.384	(0.265)
Bordering states w/bans [+]	1.405	(0.138)	1.358	(0.147)
Sodomy law [−]	−0.577	(0.216)	−0.592	(0.210)
Educational attainment [+	**0.202**	**(0.003)**	**0.205**	**(0.002)**
Population (log) [+]	0.128	(0.306)	0.128	(0.306)
Observations	1142		1142	
Log likelihood	−42.268		−42.296	

Note: *p*-values in parentheses (one-tailed tests where appropriate); expected direction of coefficient in brackets; *p*<0.1 in bold.

policies. And, consistent with the literature on political tolerance, more educated states are more likely to pass these laws.

From the descriptive comparisons, direct democracy states seem less likely than states with purely representative governments to adopt nondiscrimination policies that provide protection on the basis of sexual orientation. However, the event history analysis did not find this effect to be statistically significant.

Racial Profiling Bans

The American Civil Liberties Union defines racial profiling as "the discriminatory practice by law enforcement officials of targeting individuals for suspicion of crime based on the individual's race, ethnicity, religion or national origin."[10] Awareness of this issue was raised in 1998 by a U.S. Department of Justice investigation of the New Jersey State Police for singling out members of racial and ethnic minorities for traffic and other minor offenses in order to search them for drugs and guns.[11] Following the investigation, several states moved to adopt measures to address racial and ethnic profiling in law enforcement.

In general, states have addressed this issue through explicit bans of racial profiling practices and through data collection orders (both voluntary and mandatory). The collection of racial and ethnic data during traffic and pedestrian stops is aimed at assessing the extent of racial profiling problems, as well as monitoring law

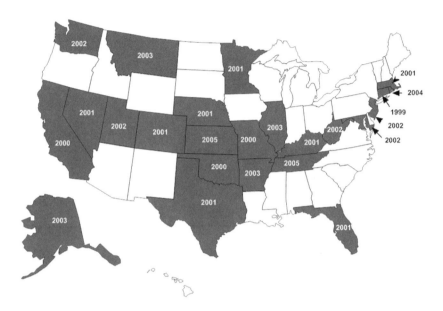

FIGURE 4.3 Adoptions of Racial Profiling Bans, 1998–2005

officers' behavior to discourage biased policing. Despite this discouragement, data collection policies do not prohibit racial profiling. These policies vary significantly across the states, with some mandating collection by all officers and others asking for voluntary collection from certain jurisdictions. The more explicit prohibitions of racial profiling tend to be more straight-forward and are much more comparable across the states. Thus, for the sake of comparability across states, I focus exclusively on explicit bans.

After the Department of Justice's investigation of the New Jersey State Police, Connecticut became the first state to adopt an explicit racial profiling ban in 1999, with three more states passing bans in 2000. In the next few years there was a flurry of adoptions, and by 2005 twenty-four states had explicitly banned racial profiling (seen in Figure 4.3). Figure 4.4 shows the yearly and cumulative patterns of adoption, with the S-shaped curve of policy diffusion evident in the cumulative adoptions line.

In the spread of racial profiling bans from 1999 to 2005, citizen legislation has not played a very discernible role. In fact, the direct effect of direct democracy has had even less of an impact on the adoption of racial profiling bans than on nondiscrimination policies that include sexual orientation. Not a single measure relating to racial profiling has qualified for a state ballot.

However, in terms of comparing the adoptions in direct democracy states to other states, there does seem to be a difference between the two sets of states. Contrary to adoptions of nondiscrimination policies that cover sexual orientation,

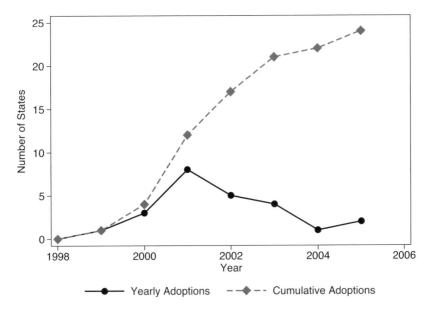

FIGURE 4.4 Adoptions of Racial Profiling Bans, 1998–2005

racial profiling bans tend to be adopted more frequently by direct democracy states. Almost 60 percent of direct democracy states had adopted an explicit racial profiling ban by 2005, while less than 40 percent of the other states had done the same. Of the twenty-four states that have adopted explicit bans, fourteen of them are direct democracy states. On the surface, it looks as if the "tyranny of the majority" argument does not hold in this case.

Event History Analyses

To examine this relationship more closely, an event history analysis is again used to assess the impact that direct democracy institutions have on the likelihood of a state adopting a racial profiling ban, given that it had not already adopted one previously. Yearly data were collected on forty-nine states from 1999 to 2005.[12] The analysis begins in 1999 with the first adoption of a state racial profiling ban by Connecticut. Due to the nature of this data, Cox proportion hazards models are employed again. The dependent variable is a dichotomous indicator of whether or not a state adopted the policy in a given year. When a state adopts its initial racial profiling ban, it is subsequently dropped from the analysis.

The independent variables in these models are the same as in the previous section, for the most part.[13] The primary variables of interest are the two measures of direct democracy institutions. The control variables include citizen ideology, party competition and control of government, education, population, and regional diffusion. The models also include a variable measuring the minority diversity of the state since racial profiling policies directly affect a wide variety of ethnic and racial minorities. This variable gauges how diverse the states' populations are in terms of African Americans, Hispanics, and Asians relative to the white population.[14] I expect that higher diversity would increase the base of support for minority protections and should increase the likelihood of the adoption of a racial profiling ban.

The estimates from the two Cox proportional hazards models are shown in Table 4.3. As with the initial comparisons, the "tyranny of the majority" argument is not supported in this case. Not only does direct democracy not inhibit the passage of these policies that protect minorities, but it also actually seems to enhance the likelihood of their passage. The Direct Democracy Impact coefficient is positive and statistically significant. This suggests that the higher the Direct Democracy Impact, the more likely the state will ban racial profiling by law enforcement agencies.

Though these results may be contrary to expectations derived from the anti-minority critiques of direct democracy, they make more sense in light of one of the key assumptions in this argument. The "tyranny of the majority" argument is essentially a special case of a more general majoritarian effect of direct democracy. It assumes that pro-minority policies would not be favored by a majority of the population, thus making these policies less likely to pass. However, for racial profiling laws this assumption does not hold. First, racial profiling affects many different minority groups that may be able to generate a broader base of support that could approach a majority. Second, in many cases the majority group may

TABLE 4.3 Adoptions of Racial Profiling Laws, 1998–2005

Variable	(1)		(2)	
	Coefficient	p-value	Coefficient	p-value
Direct democracy [–]	**1.189**	**(0.014)**	—	—
Direct Democracy Impact [–]	—	—	**0.298**	**(0.012)**
Citizen ideology [+]	–0.017	(0.322)	–0.018	(0.297)
Racial diversity [+]	–0.843	(0.633)	–0.808	(0.648)
Democratic government [+]	0.382	(0.514)	0.426	(0.476)
Republican government [–]	–1.049	(0.154)	–1.163	(0.128)
Party competition [+]	–1.648	(0.663)	–2.436	(0.529)
Bordering states w/bans [+]	–0.555	(0.682)	–0.720	(0.597)
Educational attainment [+]	**0.133**	**(0.023)**	**0.121**	**(0.035)**
Population (log) [+]	0.350	(0.222)	0.268	(0.350)
Observations	323		323	
Log likelihood	–59.266		–59.277	

Note: p-values in parentheses (one-tailed tests where appropriate); expected direction of coefficient in brackets; p<0.1 in bold.

not be "united in a common interest" against the minority groups as Madison writes in his discussion of the problems of majority factions.[15]

In the case of racial profiling, an overwhelming majority of Americans seemed to support banning the practice. In 1999, following several years of news coverage of highway stops of innocent, minority drivers, a Gallup poll found that 81 percent of respondents disapproved of racial profiling.[16] With such overwhelming support for racial profiling bans, the results from this analysis suggest that the impact of direct democracy institutions is to make government more responsive to public preferences. These results are more in line with a generalized majoritarian impact argument than a strict "tyranny of the majority" argument.

Moving down the models, the only control variable that significantly affects the likelihood of passing a racial profiling ban in a given year is educational attainment. As expected, states with more educated citizens are more likely to pass these types of policies that provide protections for minority groups. The only other control variable that approaches statistical significance is the Republican control of government variable, which shows that these governments may be less likely to pass a profiling ban.

The evidence from this examination of racial profiling bans in the American states suggests that, contrary to the "tyranny of the majority" argument, minorities may actually benefit from direct democracy institutions in some cases. In the case of racial profiling bans, which affect many minority groups and has overwhelming public opposition, direct democracy institutions seems to have increased the responsiveness of state government on this issue.

Hate Crime Laws

The previous analyses in this chapter examined two very different types of pro-minority policies that aimed to protect different minority groups. In this section, I examine another issue, hate crimes, which affects gay rights as well as the rights of racial and ethnic minorities.

The Federal Hate Crimes Statistics Act of 1990 defines hate crimes as "crimes in which the defendant's conduct was motivated by hatred, bias, or prejudice based on the actual or perceived race, color, religion, national origin, ethnicity, gender, or sexual orientation of another individual or group of individuals."[17] This differentiation in crimes based on the motivation of the perpetrator is necessary, advocates argue, because bias or hate crimes cause special injury to victims due to the knowledge that their own race (or ethnicity or religion or sexual orientation) was the prime motive for the crime committed against them. Furthermore, hate crimes can send a symbolic message of fear and terror to members of the victim's community.[18] For these reasons, hate crimes are viewed as more egregious than other crimes. States have responded by enacting hate crime laws that enhance penalties for existing crimes and/or create new categories of crimes like "ethnic intimidation" or "malicious harassment."

Although hate crimes have occurred throughout American history, the differentiation from crimes motivated by other factors is a relatively recent development. The movement to adopt hate crimes policies began at the convergence of several minority group movements, like the civil rights movement and the gay rights movement, and the victims' rights movement in the late 1960s. With this issue convergence, a broad coalition of groups pressed for government action on the issue of hate crimes. In particular, the Anti-Defamation League of B'nai B'rith (ADL) pushed for governments to adopt its model hate crime legislation—which was unveiled in 1981. That same year, Oregon and Washington became the first states to adopt a broad hate crime statute that recognized, defined, and responded to discriminatory violence.[19] While states have used various approaches to address hate crimes, from the modification of existing statutes to the creation of new and freestanding hate crime statutes, the core policy concept of enhancing penalties for these types of crimes quickly diffused to other states. By 1990, twenty-eight states had enacted a hate crime statute (see Figures 4.5 and 4.6).

The pattern of adoptions does not follow the classic s-shape, as shown in Figure 4.6, but rather there seems to be several distinct periods of policy adoptions. The first peaks in 1982 and subsides by 1985. The second peaks in 1989 and subsides by 1991. The most recent period has seen a fairly steady pattern, with a few states adopting hate crimes legislation each year until 2004. These three waves of

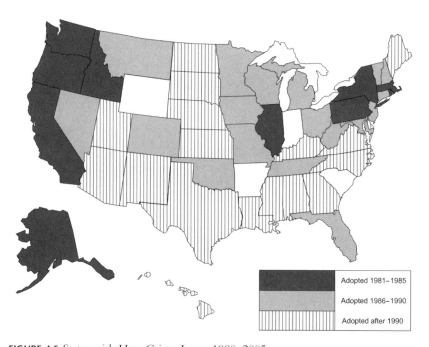

FIGURE 4.5 States with Hate Crime Laws, 1980–2005

adoption are evident in both the cumulative and yearly adoption curves. By 2007, only four states had failed to enact a hate crime law.

Like the diffusion of racial profiling bans, ballot measures have not been used to adopt hate crime laws in the United States. Thus, there does not seem to be a direct effect of direct democracy in this case. Comparing the number of adoptions in direct democracy states to non-direct democracy states also suggests no significant effect of direct democracy on the adoption of hate crime laws. Almost every state has adopted a hate crime law, regardless of the presence of direct democracy institutions. Of the four states that do not have a hate crime law, two are direct democracy states and two are non-direct democracy states.

However, by breaking down the adoptions into the three periods (1980–5, 1986–90, 1990–2005), some differences between the two types of states begin to emerge. In the first period, direct democracy states constituted seven of the ten adoptions, but in the second period they constituted only eight of the eighteen adoptions. Of the last eighteen adoptions, seven were direct democracy states. Direct democracy states were among the earliest innovators and adopters of hate crime policies (e.g., Oregon, Washington, and California), accounting for 70 percent of the initial adoptions in the 1980s. Non-direct democracy states caught up in later periods. Still, it is not clear from this examination whether the early spate of adoptions by direct democracy states was caused by these institutions or by some other policy determinant such as citizen ideology.

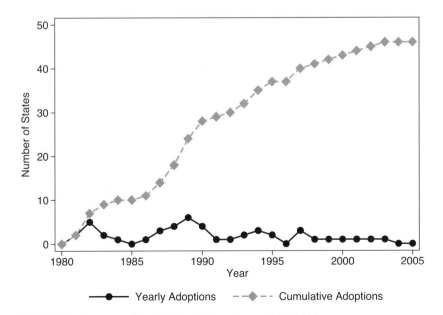

FIGURE 4.6 Adoptions of Initial Hate Crime Laws, 1980–2005

Event History Analyses

To more explicitly test the effect of direct democracy on the likelihood of a state adopting a hate crime law, while also controlling for other factors, it is once again necessary to undertake an event history analysis. As with the previous analyses, the dependent variable is a dichotomous indicator of whether or not the state adopted the policy in a given year. Once the state adopts a hate crime policy, it is subsequently dropped from the analysis. Data from forty-nine states were collected from 1981 to 2005.[20] The time period under analysis begins in 1981, when Oregon and Washington became the first states to adopt a hate crime policy. The primary explanatory variables of interest are, once again, the dichotomous indicator of direct democracy and the Direct Democracy Impact variable based on a principle components analysis of the three measures of direct democracy institutions. The rest of the independent variables follow the models from the racial profiling analysis.

The results are shown in Table 4.4. The coefficient on the Direct Democracy Impact variable shows support for the differences between the two types of states discussed above. While almost every state had adopted a hate crime law by 2005, direct democracy states show a significantly higher propensity to adopt this policy for any given year when other factors are controlled for. This relationship also holds using the Direct Democracy Impact variable. Rather than restricting minority rights, direct democracy institutions seem to help expand them in this case.

TABLE 4.4 Adoptions of Hate Crime Laws, 1981–2005

Variable	(1) Coefficient	p-value	(2) Coefficient	p-value
Direct democracy [–]	**0.822**	**(0.034)**	—	—
Direct Democracy Impact [–]	—	—	**0.184**	**(0.040)**
Citizen ideology [+]	**0.034**	**(0.025)**	**0.034**	**(0.027)**
Racial diversity [+]	−1.882	(0.129)	**−2.133**	**(0.084)**
Democratic government [+]	0.051	(0.926)	−0.021	(0.970)
Republican government [–]	−0.186	(0.700)	−0.230	(0.631)
Party competition [+]	0.380	(0.874)	0.139	(0.953)
Bordering states w/bans [+]	−0.943	(0.302)	−0.939	(0.303)
Educational attainment [+]	**0.150**	**(0.005)**	**0.149**	**(0.005)**
Population (log) [+]	**0.752**	**(0.001)**	**0.728**	**(0.002)**
Observations	567		567	
Log likelihood	−103.999		−104.219	

Note: p-values in parentheses (one-tailed tests where appropriate); expected direction of coefficient in brackets; $p<0.1$ in bold.

In addition to the effect of direct democracy, several control variables have significant impacts on a state's likelihood of adopting a hate crime law. As expected, states with larger, more educated, and more liberal populations are more likely to adopt these policies. Interestingly, party competition, regional diffusion, and racial diversity do not seem to affect the probability of passing a hate crime law as the extant literature would expect.[21]

The results from this analysis are consistent with the results from the racial profiling examination. Like the racial profiling issue, hate crime laws affect a broad range of minority groups and have a wide base of support. This base may be even wider and include members of traditional majority groups. According to the U.S. Department of Justice, almost 21 percent of hate crime victims in 1992 and just less than 20 percent in 1999 were targets of anti–white bias.[22] This is the second highest percentage of hate crime victims. The same reports show that white males constitute 40 percent of the victims in the most serious hate crimes. Beyond this wide base (and probably due to it) state hate crime laws have also received strong public support. A Gallup poll conducted in 1999 found that 70 percent of respondents would favor a hate crime law in their state. With this strong and wide-ranging support, the positive effect of direct democracy makes sense. Again, these institutions are designed to make government more responsive to the public preferences. In the cases of racial profiling and hate crime laws, policies that benefit minorities *in general*, direct democracy can help protect minority groups.

Hate Crime Laws, Sexual Orientation, and Direct Democracy

So far, the examinations of the adoptions of pro-minority policies have produced two distinct results that seem dependent on the policy issue at hand. When the policy is broadly defined to protect a wide range of minority groups (like racial profiling or hate crimes) and has popular support, direct democracy has a positive impact on the likelihood of a state adopting these types of measures. However, when the policy is more narrowly defined to protect a single, smaller minority group and subsequently receives less popular support, direct democracy may have the opposite effect and decreases the likelihood of a state adopting these policies. Again, these results fit the broader majoritarian impact of direct democracy where policies favored by the majority of the public are adopted no matter how they affect minority rights.

In this section, I test this pattern by examining hate crime policies again. In the first analysis I examined the adoption of a state's initial hate crime policy, no matter how the protected classes were defined. In this analysis, I'll narrow my focus to hate crime policies that include sexual orientation. With a sole focus on providing protections for a narrower and less publicly supported minority group, attitudes towards this policy should be less positive. If the pattern evident from the first three analyses holds, states with direct democracy institutions should be

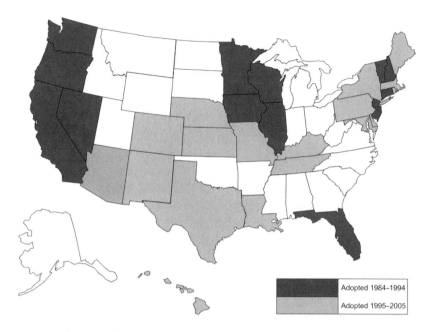

FIGURE 4.7 States with Hate Crime Laws That Include Sexual Orientation, 1984–2005

less likely to adopt hate crime policies that include sexual orientation than other states.

Hate crime policies that include crimes motivated by bias based on sexual orientation are less widespread than hate crimes policies that protect more traditional classes of groups based on race and ethnicity (see Figure 4.7). Still, by 2005, there were thirty-one states with hate crime laws that cover crimes motivated by a victim's sexual orientation. Many of the earliest states to adopt hate crime policies did not include sexual orientation in their initial policy, but most added it later on. The first state to adopt a hate crime policy that included sexual orientation was California in 1984. As seen in Figure 4.8, twelve more states followed in the next decade by adding sexual orientation to their existing hate crime law or by including this class of crimes in their initial policy. A second wave of adoptions followed from 1995 to 2005, punctuated by the high-profile killing of Matthew Shepard, a gay student at the University of Wyoming, in 1998. From 1995 to 2005, thirteen more states included sexual orientation in their hate crime laws. Interestingly, Wyoming, a state with direct democracy institutions, is one of the few states without a hate crime law, much less one that covers sexual orientation.

Of the thirty-one states with hate crime policies that include sexual orientation, twelve are direct democracy states. Only half of the direct democracy states have

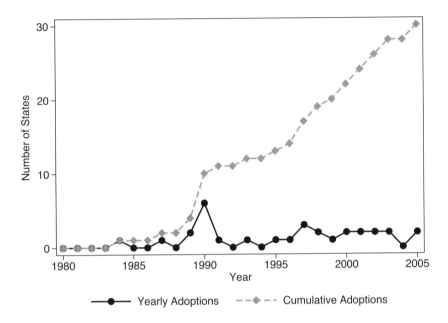

FIGURE 4.8 Adoptions of Hate Crime Laws That Include Sexual Orientation, 1980–2005

adopted this policy, while nearly 70 percent of non-direct democracy states have done the same. Thus, on the surface it looks as if direct democracy states are less likely to adopt this more narrow pro-minority policy, but obviously further testing is necessary before any conclusions can be drawn.

Event History Analyses

To further test this difference between direct democracy states and non-direct democracy states, I estimate two Cox proportional hazards models. Data on forty-nine states from 1984 to 2005 were collected.[23] The dependent variable in this analysis is a dichotomous indicator of whether a state adopted a hate crime policy that includes sexual orientation in a given year. Once a state adopts the policy it is subsequently dropped from the analysis. The primary independent variables are the two measures of direct democracy institutions used throughout the study.

The other independent variables are the same as the models from the analysis of nondiscrimination policies covering sexual orientation. In addition, a dichotomous indicator of whether a state had previously adopted a general hate crime law is included. A state with an existing hate crime law must act to grant these protections exclusively to homosexuals, and thus the policy proposal is focused solely on the rights of a single group. When a state does not have an existing hate crime law, its consideration of a measure that covers sexual orientation is focused simultaneously on several other groups. For this reason, states that already have a hate crime law that does not include sexual orientation should be less likely to adopt the policy in question.

The results from the two Cox proportional hazards models are presented in Table 4.5. In this case, both direct democracy coefficients are statistically indistinguishable from zero. This suggests that, as in the case of nondiscrimination policy covering sexual orientation, direct democracy does not seem to affect the likelihood of a state adopting a policy to cover sexual orientation under its hate crimes statute. Again, this may reflect the contrasting popular support for hate crime policies and the opposition to homosexuality and gay rights. Given these ambivalent public attitudes towards this policy, there may be no clear majority to which direct democracy institutions can provide increased responsiveness.

Many of the other independent variables, however, show significant effects. As expected, states with Republican-controlled governments and higher numbers of evangelicals are less likely to pass this policy. In addition, states with an existing hate crime policy are less likely to expand the policy to include sexual orientation. This is consistent with the conflicting support for hate crime laws and opposition to gay rights. For positive impacts, larger states, and Democratic-controlled governments are more likely to adopt these measures. Surprisingly, liberal states show a significant negative effect on passing these hate crime laws.

TABLE 4.5 Adoptions of Hate Crime Laws That Include Sexual Orientation

Variable	(1) Coefficient	p-value	(2) Coefficient	p-value
Direct democracy [–]	0.245	(0.630)	—	—
Direct Democracy Impact [–]	—	—	0.115	(0.369)
Citizen ideology [+]	**−0.067**	**(0.009)**	**−0.067**	**(0.010)**
Evangelical rate [–]	**−0.153**	**(0.002)**	**−0.155**	**(0.002)**
Same-sex households [+]	1.869	(0.123)	1.832	(0.127)
Democratic government [+]	**1.404**	**(0.017)**	**1.482**	**(0.013)**
Republican government [–]	**−1.564**	**(0.072)**	**−1.596**	**(0.065)**
Party competition [+]	3.010	(0.351)	3.105	(0.336)
Bordering states w/bans [+]	1.207	(0.236)	1.300	(0.206)
Sodomy law [–]	0.075	(0.886)	0.081	(0.877)
Existing hate crime law [–]	**−1.006**	**(0.059)**	**−1.052**	**(0.045)**
Educational attainment [+]	0.018	(0.736)	0.014	(0.796)
Population (log) [+]	**0.483**	**(0.046)**	**0.477**	**(0.044)**
Observations	951		951	
Log likelihood	−68.871		−68.588	

Note: p-values in parentheses (one-tailed tests where appropriate); expected direction of coefficient in brackets; $p<0.1$ in bold.

This may reflect the tendency of the most liberal states to be early adopters of general hate crime laws.

In assessing the impact of direct democracy on the adoption of hate crime policies that cover crimes motivated by a victim's sexual orientation, the evidence points to a null effect. There is neither a negative nor positive impact that reflects any increased responsiveness to the majority preferences in this case. This may be due to public ambivalence about this issue. On the one hand, the very term "hate crime" engenders public support for these types of policies, with general hate crime policies receiving wide public backing. On the other hand, including sexual orientation means extending this policy to cover a minority group that traditionally has received very little public acceptance or support.

Discussion

In the analyses of the adoption of pro-minority policies, the impact of direct democracy has varied across the different policies. While the "tyranny of the majority" argument would predict a negative effect for all four policies, this expectation was not met for any of the pro-minority policies. Instead the chapter revealed two pro-minority policies—racial profiles bans and hate crime laws—where direct democracy actually increased the likelihood of adoption. These results, given the broad scope and the national popularity of the two policies, were suggestive of a more general majoritarian effect. When pro-minority policies are able to draw on a wider base of support, as in the cases of racial profiling bans and general hate crime laws, direct democracy can aid in protecting the rights of minority groups.

The variation in the impact of direct democracy on the adoption of pro-minority policies evident in this chapter makes it clear that pro-minority policies have different dynamics than anti-minority policies. Where the anti-minority policies experienced a consistent negative effect on minority rights in direct democracy states, pro-minority policies tend to have a more general majoritarian effect that does not necessarily always endanger the rights of minorities. On balance, this creates situations where policy outcomes are biased against the rights of minorities. Though minority groups can, in some cases, win civil rights protections under direct democracy institutions, they have little recourse when their rights are targeted. The majoritarian effects of direct democracy place the rights of minority groups at the whim of majority attitudes. In examining these four pro-minority policies, two of the analyses revealed an increase in pro-minority outcomes for direct democracy states that is consistent with a majoritarian effect. Unfortunately, without state-level measures of issue attitudes, this argument is difficult to address more closely.

Clearly, more work on these issues is needed, especially studies that focus on the interaction between public preferences on particular pro-minority policies and direct democracy institutions. Still, the analyses from this chapter did shed some light on this subject matter. It is apparent that the dynamics of pro-minority policy adoption are highly variable and may be contingent on factors like citizen ideology, public perceptions of the policy, and the organizational strength of the groups involved. This chapter also makes clear that the politics of pro-minority policies are different from anti-minority policies, where more consistent impacts of direct democracy are apparent.

5

CONCLUSION

Although concern over the rights of minority groups has long been part of the debate on direct democracy institutions, the existing scholarly literature has yet to produce systematic and empirical evidence to either validate or contradict this argument. Indeed, previous research has generated findings that seem to support both sides of the debate depending on the study. On the whole, this line of research has presented a very mixed picture of how direct democracy affects policies that impact the rights of minority groups. On the one hand, some work has shown what appear to be tyrannical outcomes that produce anti-minority policies. On the other hand, there is work that suggests that these outcomes are not more prevalent under direct democracy institutions.

As discussed earlier, the ambiguous results of most of the literature that address this question are due to two critical limitations. First, they tend to only focus on the direct effects of direct democracy: on the policy outcomes of ballot initiatives and popular referenda. This approach does not account for the indirect effects of direct democracy that would manifest themselves in outcomes from traditional legislation in direct democracy states. In order to get a complete picture of the impact of direct democracy on the rights of minorities (or any other policy area for that matter), it is necessary to examine both citizen and traditional legislations.

The second limitation of the existing research, which has led to such a murky view of the impact of direct democracy on minority rights, is the tendency for these studies to solely focus on states with direct democracy institutions. The "tyranny of the majority" argument is a comparative critique. The claim is that representative democratic systems are better able to protect minority rights than systems with direct democracy institutions. So in order to evaluate whether this claim is correct, it is necessary to directly compare policy decisions in the two types of institutional arrangements.

Taken together, these two extensions—accounting for both direct and indirect effects, and comparing direct democracy states with states without direct democracy institutions—provide for a more comprehensive understanding of the impact of citizen legislative institutions have on minority rights.

Summary of Findings

Utilizing these two critical extensions, the analyses in Chapters 2 and 3 produced consistent and clear results that support the anti-minority critique of direct democracy institutions. Chapter 2 examined the effect of direct democracy on the adoption of three explicitly anti-minority policies: same-sex marriage bans, Official English laws, and affirmative action bans. The first set of analyses found that states with direct democracy institutions were significantly more likely to adopt same-sex marriage bans in a given year than non-direct democracy states. Furthermore, the event history analyses of the adoption of same-sex marriage bans revealed that the variation in states' direct democracy institutional arrangements also had an impact on policy adoption. The index of Direct Democracy Impact suggests that states with more insulated legislatures, more stringent qualification requirements, and that use initiative less often are better able to protect the rights of minority groups.

This anti-minority effect was also apparent in the examination of Official English laws. Following the previous literature on Official English, the event history analyses showed that, among states with high numbers of foreign-born residents, those with direct democracy were more likely to adopt this restrictive language policy.[1] When language policy is a salient issue because the majority feels threatened by the prevalence of foreign languages in their state, direct democracy institutions seem to make government more responsive to this perceived threat. Put more succinctly, when the majority prefers a restrictive language policy, direct democracy institutions increase the probability of state governments adopting an Official English law.

The results of the analyses of affirmative action bans were also consistent with the "tyranny of the majority" argument. Only states with direct democracy institutions have adopted this broad anti-minority measure. Meanwhile, states without direct democracy institutions, like New Jersey, have considered this policy but have been unable to pass it, suggesting that the filtering mechanisms of representative democracy were helping to protect minority rights. Though not one non–direct democracy state has adopted an affirmative action ban to date, a third of the direct democracy states have passed this policy.

The third chapter examined individual anti-minority policy proposals and their rates of passage. Again, by examining both traditional and citizen legislation, and comparing outcomes across institutional arrangements, the impact of direct democracy was clear and consistent. Direct democracy states had significantly higher rates of passage for policy proposals that targeted the rights of homosexuals, speakers of foreign languages, and minorities in general. Furthermore, the probability of passing any individual anti-minority policy proposal was significantly higher in states with direct initiatives. The effects of the arrangements of direct democracy institutions are also evident from this analysis. Policy proposals in states with less insulated legislatures, easier qualification requirements, and higher initiative use all had higher probabilities of passage.

The analyses from Chapters 2 and 3 all produced clear evidence showing that the rights of minority group were at higher risk in direct democracy states than in states without citizen legislative institutions. These policies, whether they target homosexuals, speakers of foreign languages, or broadly apply to all minorities, have a higher probability of passing in direct democracy states and thus the rights of minorities are at heightened jeopardy in these states.

However, anti-minority policies are not the only policies that affect the rights of minority groups. States can also pass legislation to protect minority rights. Little research has focused on the effect that direct democracy has on the adoption of these pro-minority policies. The fourth chapter examined four pro-minority policies—nondiscrimination laws that include sexual orientation, racial profiling bans, hate crime laws, and hate crime laws that cover sexual orientation—to ascertain the impact of direct democracy on the adoption of laws that would enhance or protect the rights of minority groups. The results from these analyses found little support for the argument that direct democracy institutions have a negative impact on the adoption of pro-minority policies. For two of the four analyses, direct democracy did not have a statistically significant impact on the adoption of the pro-minority policy. The likelihood of a state adopting a racial profiling ban or a hate crime law was positively affected by direct democracy institutions.

Given the consistent results from the analyses of anti-minority policies in support of the "tyranny of the majority" argument, the varied effects of direct democracy on the adoption of pro-minority policies may seem surprising. However, it is important to carefully consider the roots of this critique. Concern for minority rights under direct democracy institutions stems from the fear that government will be overly responsive to majority preferences to restrict minority rights. Embedded in this argument is the assumption that the majority will prefer policies that restrict minority rights. Again, Madison recognizes this caveat when he argues that minority rights will be endangered by pure democracy "if a majority be united in common interest."[2] Further, the assumption that public opinion runs counter to the interests of minority groups is integrated into the empirical analyses presented here.

Thus, it is appropriate to consider that the "tyranny of the majority" argument is a special case of a more general effect of direct democracy—a majoritarian effect where governments increase their responsiveness to the preferences of the majority. When the majority of the public is united against a minority group, the rights of this minority are placed at higher risk under direct democracy institutions than under representative democratic institutions. But when the majority of the public is not united against a minority group, we should not expect direct democracy to endanger the rights of that minority group. Further, we should expect that, in cases where the majority actually prefers to protect the rights of a minority group, it is more likely that pro-minority policies will be enacted.

Public Preferences and Direct Democracy

In order to further explore whether the more general majoritarian effect of direct democracy can help explain the results of the previous analyses, it is necessary to examine public preferences on these issues. If direct democracy institutions have broad majoritarian effects, rather than a strict anti-minority effect, then public support for a policy should be associated with a positive impact of these institutions on policy adoption. Likewise, lack of public support for a policy should be associated with a negative impact on adoption. Ideally, this could be tested by incorporating annual, state-level measures of public attitudes towards the policy in question into the event history models as an interaction term with the direct democracy variables.

Though great strides have been made in recent years in developing measures of state-level public opinion, annual estimates of issue-specific attitudes are not yet available. Measuring state-level public opinion presents challenges because state-specific surveys tend to vary in their questions across the fifty states and across different years. National surveys, meanwhile, are not designed to be representative of each state and often do not have respondents from all fifty states. Thus, we cannot directly measure state public opinion in all fifty states with national surveys. Less direct approaches, such as aggregating national surveys and inferring public attitudes based on the behavior of elected officials, have been able to provide good estimates of more general attitudes (e.g., ideological identification and public mood), but these approaches rely on aggregating data on a variety of issues that make estimating specific attitudes quite difficult.[3] More recently, Multilevel Regression and Poststratification (MRP) techniques have allowed scholars to estimate state-level public opinion without relying on as much aggregation of surveys.[4] This allows for measurement of specific issue attitudes, like support for same-sex marriage. However, MRP estimates rely on questions from national surveys and these surveys often do not ask about the same issue year after year. So, if issue attitudes change over time, MRP approaches often cannot account for this variation. Issue attitudes tend to be much more dynamic than general ideological orientations and partisan identification. Thus, using static measures of issue attitudes would risk biasing the results of dynamic analyses such as event history analysis.

An alternative approach relies on proxy measures of the public's attitudes toward each policy. In essence, this approach is taken in the analysis of the adoption of Official English laws in the second chapter. Based on the minority threat theory, the public should be more in favor of a restrictive language policy, like an Official English law, as the number of foreign-language speakers in their state increases. The incorporation of the percent of each state's population that is foreign born in the model acts as a proxy measure for public attitudes towards language policy. Using this specification, it is clear that states with direct democracy institutions were more responsive to the majority's preferences for this type of policy. By indirectly accounting for the public issue attitudes, the analysis was able to demonstrate the majoritarian effects of direct democracy institutions, even in a case where public opinion on the issue varied quite a bit from state to state. The difficulty in this approach is finding suitable proxy measures that could be used to approximate public preferences on each of the policies under examination here.

National-Level Issue Attitudes and Direct Democracy

Another way to examine the interplay of public preferences and the impact of direct democracy institutions on policy adoption is to compare the results of the previous analyses with national-level public opinion on these policies. Although this approach cannot account for state-level variations in issue attitudes, it does provide a starting point from which to evaluate the varying impacts of direct democracy across different minority rights policies.

Figure 5.1 shows the percent of respondents that have attitudes in line with the anti-minority policies analyzed in the second chapter.[5] From 1994 to 2008,

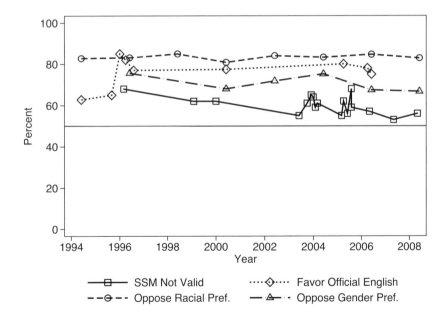

FIGURE 5.1 National-Level Issue Attitudes Related to Anti-Minority Policies

TABLE 5.1 National-Level Issue Attitudes and Direct Democracy Effects

Policy	Average public support (%)	Direct democracy effects	
		Policy adoption	Minority rights
Anti-minority policies			
Same-sex marriage ban	60.2	+	−
Official English	75.8	+	-
Affirmative action ban	83.3 (race)		-
	70.8 (gender)	+	-
Pro-minority policies			
Nondiscrimination law w/sexual orientation	54.4★	No effect	No effect
Hate crime laws	67.8	+	+
Hate crime laws w/sexual orientation	56★	No effect	No effect
Racial profiling ban	75	+	+

Notes: Wording of survey questions is shown in the Appendix.

★ Over the same time period, however, only 21.8% of respondents agreed that "homosexuality is not wrong."

Sources: Gallup Poll 2000–6, General Social Survey 1982–2006, Washington Post/Kaiser Family Foundation/Harvard University, September 2000.

a clear majority of Americans believed that marriages between homosexuals should not be recognized by law as valid. On average during this time period, over 60 percent of Americans opposed same-sex marriage. The graph also shows that more than three-quarters of Americans, on average, favor making English the official language of the United States. Finally, Figure 5.1 demonstrates that relatively large majorities of Americans oppose race- or gender-based preferences in hiring.

In terms of the anti-minority policies examined in Chapter 2, it is evident that there are large majorities of Americans that support these policies. This high level of support also tends to be consistent over time. On their own, these public opinion data support both a strict "tyranny of the majority" argument and a more general majoritarian argument. As seen in Table 5.1, the majority support for each of the anti-minority policies is associated with a negative impact on the likelihood of a state adopting these policies in a given year. Since these policies each restrict minority rights, this positive effect on policy adoption has a negative impact on the rights of these minority groups. Thus, there is majoritarian effect where direct democracy institutions increase responsiveness to the majority's preferences, but there is also an anti-minority effect where direct democracy institutions are associated with the adoption of policies that restrict minority rights.

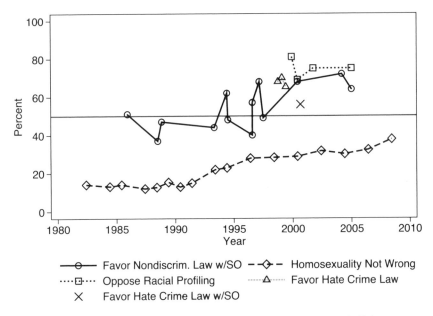

FIGURE 5.2 National-Level Issue Attitudes Related to Pro-Minority Policies

Public opinion pertaining to the pro-minority policies that were examined in Chapter 4 shows a bit more variation (see Figure 5.2).[6] While attitudes towards homosexuality have become more positive since 1982 according to the General Social Survey, a large majority continues to believe that it is "wrong" to some extent. Between 1982 and 2008, the average percent of Americans that responded that homosexuality is "not wrong at all" is under 22 percent, with a low of 12 percent in 1987 and high of 37 percent in 2008. At the same time, attitudes toward nondiscrimination laws covering sexual orientation are more supportive, but they do not reach consistent majority levels until the end of the time period examined here. Thus, Americans' attitudes toward protecting the Lesbian, Gay, Bisexual, and Transgender (LGBT) community from discrimination seem to be quite ambivalent.

Attitudes towards hate crime laws, meanwhile, are more consistently supportive. In 1998 and 1999, national polls found that two-thirds of Americans, on average, would support the adoption of laws to increase penalties for crimes targeting victims as members of racial and ethnic minority groups. Unfortunately, this question was not asked in subsequent years in most national polls. Even fewer comparable questions asked about hate crime laws and sexual orientation, but one poll did find that 56 percent of Americans favor these policies. As in the case of nondiscrimination laws covering sexual orientation, this middling support for these types of hate crime laws should be viewed in contrast to the low percentage of

Americans that find nothing wrong with homosexuality. Finally, opposition to racial profiling averaged three-quarters of respondents across four polls from 1999 to 2005.

Along with the variation in public support for these pro-minority policies, a corresponding variation in the effects of direct democracy on policy adoption is also evident (see Table 5.1). Despite such negative attitudes towards homosexuality, states with direct democracy institutions were not significantly less likely to adopt a nondiscrimination law covering sexual orientation. This null effect may reflect the conflicted nature of public opinion on this issue. On the one hand, the majority does not approve of homosexuality. On the other hand, Americans seem to support policies that protect civil rights.

The next two pro-minority policies, however, do not fit a strict "tyranny of the majority" argument. Despite protecting minority rights, hate crime laws actually enjoy broad support among Americans. Given the strong support of the majority for this policy, direct democracy institutions may marginally increase the likelihood of adopting a state hate crime law as would be predicted by a general majoritarian argument. Direct democracy institutions actually show a marginally positive, not negative, impact on the rights of minorities in the case of hate crime laws. The association between attitudes towards racial profiling and the impact of direct democracy institutions lends itself to a similar conclusion. In response to majority opposition to racial profiling, direct democracy institutions increase the probability of adopting a racial profiling ban. In this case there is a majoritarian effect, but not the anti-minority impact predicted by a strict "tyranny of the majority" argument.

Interpretation of the association between public support for hate crime laws that apply to crimes motivated by the victim's sexual orientation and the impact of direct democracy is less straight-forward. While there is majority support for this policy, there was no corresponding significant effect of direct democracy on policy adoption and subsequently no discernible impact on the rights of homosexuals. This result, similar to the ones from the nondiscrimination policies, may be reflective of the ambiguous nature of public opinion regarding this issue. While a large majority of Americans support hate crime laws, a similarly large majority hold negative attitudes towards homosexuality. Without a clear majority preference on this policy, the majoritarian effect of direct democracy may be mitigated.

In all, the evidence presented in Table 5.1 supports the more general majoritarian effect of direct democracy. Although the survey data presented here are national-level data, they nonetheless provide compelling support for a more generalizable majoritarian impact of direct democracy than for a narrower, anti-minority impact of these institutions. Only three of the seven policies showed an anti-minority effect, compared with five that clearly showed a majoritarian effect. And, in the cases of nondiscrimination and hate crime laws that include sexual orientation, there is evidence that the insignificant effects of direct democracy may be due to ambiguity in public preferences.

Conclusion

Viewing the results of the previous chapters through a lens of public preferences strongly suggests the effect of direct democracy on the adoption of policies that pertain to the rights of minority groups is a majoritarian effect that should be generalizable to all types of policies. That is, direct democracy institutions should increase the likelihood of states adopting policies that have majority public support and should also decrease the probability of adopting policies that have majority opposition. Obviously, this broader majoritarian effect needs to be further scrutinized and tested before any hard conclusions can be drawn, but the initial evidence presented on minority rights policies here does fit this argument well.

Although the analyses in this study are more supportive of a majoritarian effect than a strict "tyrannical" effect, this does not mean that the impact of direct democracy on minority rights is negligible or even positive. Rather, the analyses have shown that in many cases the resulting policy has a negative impact on minority rights. All of the anti-minority policies under examination here had an increased probability of adoption in states with direct democracy. This impact is evident from Table 5.2, which shows each state's adoption record on the policies considered in this study. Only states with direct initiatives adopted all three anti-minority policies. Of the twenty-four direct democracy states, only Massachusetts did not pass any of the three contemporary anti-minority policies considered here. Meanwhile, five of the non-direct democracy states did not adopt any one of these policies, and none of these states adopted all three. These differences were also apparent from the analyses of anti-minority bill passage in Chapter 3.

For pro-minority policies, direct democracy had a positive impact for two policies and insignificant impacts on two others. This variation in effects seems to be contingent on public preferences, or the extent to which the majority is "united in common interest" against a minority. As opposed to the anti-minority policies, the varying impacts of direct democracy create a muddled picture of the overall impact of direct democracy on minority rights in terms of the adoption of pro-minority policies. Table 5.3 shows the adoptions of the four pro-minority policies examined in this study. There is no clear difference between the two types of states. Each includes several states that adopt all of the policies, as well as a few states that have adopted none.

Comparing the patterns visibly evident in Tables 5.2 and 5.3 further supports the argument that direct democracy has had a detrimental impact on minority rights. The presence of direct democracy institutions is moderately correlated with higher numbers of anti-minority policies adopted—0.36 for all direct democracy states and 0.44 for states with direct initiatives—suggesting a strong relationship between these policies and direct democracy. Meanwhile, the correlations between states with direct democracy institutions and the number of pro-minority policy adoptions show virtually no relationship: 0.10 for all direct democracy states and 0.04 for direct initiative states.

TABLE 5.2 Anti-Minority Policies Adopted from 1980 to 2008

State	SS ban	Official English	AA ban	Total	Direct initiatives
Direct democracy states					
CA	▲	▲	▲	3	▲
CO	▲	▲	▲	3	▲
FL	▲	▲	▲	3	▲
MO	▲	▲	▲	3	▲
UT	▲	▲	▲	3	▲
AK	▲	▲		2	
AZ	▲	▲		2	▲
AR	▲	▲		2	▲
MS	▲	▲		2	
MT	▲	▲		2	▲
ND	▲	▲		2	▲
SD	▲	▲		2	▲
MI	▲		▲	2	▲
NE	▲	★	▲	2	▲
WA	▲		▲	2	▲
ID	▲			1	▲
IL	▲	★		1	▲
ME	▲			1	
NV	▲			1	▲
OH	▲			1	▲
OK	▲			1	▲
OR	▲			1	▲
WY		▲		1	
MA				0	
Non-direct democracy states					
AL	▲	▲		2	
GA	▲	▲		2	
IN	▲	▲		2	
IA	▲	▲		2	
KY	▲	▲		2	
NH	▲	▲		2	
NC	▲	▲		2	
SC	▲	▲		2	
TN	▲	▲		2	
VA	▲	▲		2	
CT	▲			1	
DE	▲			1	
HI	▲	★		1	
KS	▲			1	
LA	▲	★		1	
MN	▲			1	
PA	▲			1	
TX	▲			1	
VT	▲			1	
WV	▲			1	
WI	▲			1	
MD				0	
NJ				0	
NM		★		0	
NY				0	
RI				0	

Note: ★passed a symbolic or bilingual official language law prior to 1980.

TABLE 5.3 Pro-Minority Policies Adopted from 1980 to 2008

State	Hate crime law	Hate crime law—sexual orientation	Profiling ban	Non-discrimination law—sexual orientation	Total	Direct initiatives
Direct democracy states						
CA	▲	▲	▲	▲	4	▲
CO	▲	▲	▲	▲	4	▲
IL	▲	▲	▲	▲	4	▲
MA	▲	▲	▲	▲	4	
NV	▲	▲	▲	▲	4	▲
WA	▲	▲	▲	▲	4	▲
FL	▲	▲	▲		3	▲
MO	▲	▲	▲		3	▲
NE	▲	▲	▲		3	▲
ME	▲	▲		▲	3	
OR	▲	▲		▲	3	▲
AK	▲		▲		2	
MT	▲		▲		2	▲
OK	▲		▲		2	▲
UT	▲		▲		2	▲
AZ	▲				1	▲
ID	▲				1	▲
MI	▲				1	▲
MS	▲				1	
OH	▲				1	▲
SD	▲				1	▲
AR			▲		1	▲
ND					0	▲
WY					0	
Non-direct democracy states						
CT	▲	▲	▲	▲	4	
MD	▲	▲	▲	▲	4	
MN	▲	▲	▲	▲	4	
NJ	▲	▲	▲	▲	4	
RI	▲	▲	▲	▲	4	
KS	▲	▲	▲		3	
KY	▲	▲	▲		3	
TN	▲	▲	▲		3	
TX	▲	▲	▲		3	
HI	▲	▲		▲	3	
IA	▲	▲		▲	3	
NH	▲	▲		▲	3	
NM	▲	▲		▲	3	
NY	▲	▲		▲	3	
VT	▲	▲		▲	3	
WI	▲	▲		▲	3	
DE	▲	▲			2	
LA	▲	▲			2	
PA	▲	▲			2	
WV	▲		▲		2	
AL	▲				1	
GA	▲				1	
NC	▲				1	
VA	▲				1	
IN					0	
SC					0	

These associations are reflected in comparisons of the average number of policies passed between the two groups of states. For anti-minority policies, direct democracy states average significantly more adoptions than non-direct democracy states: 1.8 compared with 1.2. For pro-minority policies, there is no statistically significant difference between the two types of groups. Non-direct democracy states average 2.5 pro-minority policy adoptions while direct democracy states average 2.3 adoptions. Taken together, this suggests that the net impact of the relationships between direct democracy and the adoption of policies that affect the rights of minority groups is negative.

Again, while the effect of direct democracy on minority rights seems to be conditional on whether the majority opposes minority rights, I cannot overstate the risk that this contingency presents. Though these "tyrannical" outcomes and anti-minority effects of direct democracy can be described as a special case of a broader, majoritarian effect, this special case is far from rare. U.S. history is littered with cases in which there is strong and sometimes violent opposition to the rights of a variety of minority groups. In contemporary politics, "tyrannical outcomes," especially for policies that target homosexuals, are relatively common. This research suggests that, in these cases, minority rights are put at further risk under governmental systems with direct democracy institutions than under purely representative democratic systems.

The results from this study not only showed a strong majoritarian and often anti-minority impact of direct democracy, but also highlighted the influence that institutional arrangements of these institutions can have on public policy. This speaks directly to the previous literature. Frey and Goette concluded that the relatively few instances of anti-minority outcomes in Switzerland were a result of the benign impact of direct democracy on minority rights, but this research suggests that these results were more likely due to the arrangements of direct democracy in that country.[7] The Swiss system requires initiatives to be presented to the legislature before reaching the ballot. The legislative assembly is then given up to four years to deliberate and respond, usually offering a competing measure for public consideration. More often than not, the assembly's counter-proposal is passed rather than the public's proposal. In short, Swiss direct democracy insulates the legislature to a much higher degree than U.S. direct democracy and allows for much more deliberation and other types of filtering mechanisms. Rather than using the Swiss institutions as an example of the benign effect of direct democracy on minority groups, they are better suited as examples of how incorporating filtering mechanisms, especially legislative insulation, into direct democracy arrangements can protect minorities.

Another implication of this research pertains to the organization and mobilization of minority groups. Under traditional, representative democratic systems, minority groups seem to have a better chance at opposing restrictive policies solely through organization within their own community and by gaining representation in state legislatures. In direct democracy states, however, this tactic may not be sufficient. Minority groups may need to broaden their base of support beyond their members and aim their messages at the general public in order to build mass support for the protection of their rights. With direct democracy increasing responsiveness to public opinion, minority groups cannot just rely on representation in the legislative process. Rather, they'll need to show public support in order to better protect and enhance their interests.

In practice, this is often easier said than done. In the case of affirmative action bans, minority coalition groups such as By Any Means Necessary (BAMN) sought to widen their public support beyond racial and ethnic minorities to include women's groups. Though gender was emphasized in their public campaigns, opponents of affirmative action bans have been unable to garner the numbers necessary to form a majority. Despite tactics aimed at building a cohesive majority to oppose affirmative action bans, the public still preferred the anti-minority position.

Thus, when the rights of minority groups are contingent on majority preferences, as is the case in under direct democracy institutions, these rights are clearly at risk. Though the impact of direct democracy on minority rights is better characterized as a general majoritarian one, rather than a strict tyrannical one, the analyses presented in this study show a strong potential for policy outcomes that restrict the rights of minorities. Indeed, every anti-minority policy under examination here had a higher likelihood of being adopted in states that allowed citizen legislation. So while there are certainly some caveats in answering the question of whether direct democracy endangers minority rights, most often this question should be answered in the affirmative.

APPENDIX

National-Level Public Opinion Surveys, Question Wording

Regarding Anti-Minority Policies

Same-sex marriage ban:
- Do you think marriages between homosexuals should or should not be recognized by the law as valid, with the same rights as traditional marriages?
  - Gallup Polls, 1996–2008

Official English:
- Do you favor a law making English the official language of the United States, meaning government business would be conducted in English only, or do you oppose such a law?
  - General Social Survey, 1994
- Do you think there should be a law making English the official language of this country, or don't you feel that way?
  - *Time*/CNN/Yankelovich Partners Poll, September 1995
- I'm going to read you some proposals that are now being discussed nationally. As I read each one, please select the number that best expresses how much you favor or oppose it (strongly oppose—point 1, neutral—point 4, strongly favor—point 7). If you don't really care about the issue, please say so.) . . . Making English the official language of the United States.
  - Survey of American Political Culture, January 1996
- Suppose that on Election Day this year you could vote on key issues as well as candidates. Please tell me whether you would vote for or against each one of the following propositions. . . . A law establishing English as the official language of the United States.
  - Gallup Poll, April 1996

- Would you favor or oppose passing a law making English the official language of the United States?
  - PSRA/*Newsweek* Poll, August 1996
- Do you favor a law making English the official language of the United States, or do you oppose such a law?
  - General Social Survey, 2000
- Do you favor or oppose passing a law making English the official language of the United States?
  - *FOX News*/Opinion Dynamics Poll, 2005–6
- Do you favor a law making English the official language of the United States, or do you oppose such a law?
  - CNN Poll, June 2006

Affirmative action ban:
- Some people say that because of past discrimination, blacks should be given preference in hiring and promotion. Others say that such preference in hiring and promotion of blacks is wrong because it discriminates against whites. What about your opinion—are you for or against preferential hiring and promotion of blacks?
  - General Social Survey, 1994–2008
- Some people say that because of past discrimination, women should be given preference in hiring and promotion. Others say that such preference in hiring and promotion of women is wrong because it discriminates against men. What about your opinion—are you for or against preferential hiring and promotion of women?
  - General Social Survey, 1996–2008

Regarding Pro-Minority Policies

Non-discrimination law including sexual orientation:
- Do you favor or oppose laws to protect homosexuals against job discrimination?
  - *Los Angeles Times* Poll, 1985, 2000, 2004
- Should a federal law be passed protecting homosexuals from discrimination?
  - *CBS News/New York Times* Poll, July 1988
- Do you favor or oppose laws to protect homosexuals against job discrimination? (If favor, ask:) Do you favor such laws strongly or not strongly? (If oppose, ask:) Do you oppose such laws strongly or not strongly?
  - American National Election Study 1988 (Post-Election), November 1988

- Thinking about the issue of gay rights—do you favor or oppose extending current civil rights laws to prohibit discrimination against gay and lesbian people? (If choice is made, ask:) Is that strongly or somewhat (yes/no)?
  - *U.S. News & World Report* Poll, May 1993

- I am going to read you a list of proposals, and for each one, please tell me if you strongly favor, somewhat favor, somewhat oppose, or strongly oppose that proposal? . . . Enacting laws that would give gays and lesbians legal protection against discrimination.
  - *NBC News/Wall Street Journal* Poll, July 1994

- Now I'd like to ask you some questions about homosexuals—or gays and lesbians as they are sometimes called. Do you favor or oppose the passage of equal rights laws to protect homosexuals against job discrimination?
  - *Time*/CNN/Yankelovich Partners Poll, June 1994

- Do you agree or disagree with the following statements? . . . Homosexual Americans should not be guaranteed protection from discrimination. (If agree/disagree, ask:) Is that strongly or somewhat agree/disagree?
  - *ABC News/Washington Post* Poll, August 1996

- These days, do you think it is necessary to have laws to protect homosexuals from discrimination in hiring and promotion, or don't you think it's necessary?
  - *CBS News/New York Times* Poll, August 1996

- There are currently no federal laws protecting gays and lesbians in the workplace. Only nine states now have laws protecting gays and lesbians from workplace discrimination, and a lesbian or gay man can be fired for being gay in the other 41 states. The Employment Non-Discrimination Act, which is currently being considered in Congress, would extend civil rights and prevent job discrimination against gays and lesbians. Would you favor or oppose this law? (If favor or oppose, ask:) Is that strongly favor/oppose or somewhat favor/oppose?
  - Tarrance Group Poll, April 1997

- Do you think the government should prevent discrimination against gays in employment?
  - New Democratic Electorate Survey, July 1997

- Next, I'd like your opinion on some gay rights issues. Do you think there should or should not be laws to protect gays and lesbians from prejudice and discrimination in job opportunities?
  - National Conference for Community and Justice; Taking America's Pulse III—Intergroup Relations Survey, January 2005

- What about sexual relations between two adults of the same sex—do you think it is always wrong, almost always wrong, wrong only sometimes, or not wrong at all?
  - General Social Survey, 1982–2008

Racial profiling ban:

- Do you approve or disapprove of the use of "racial profiling" by police?
  - Gallup Poll, December 9, 1999
- Should police be prohibited from taking race in account when targeting people as suspects?
  - Democratic Leadership Council, June 2000
- It has been reported that some police officers stop motorists of certain racial or ethnic groups because the officers believe that these groups are more likely than others to commit certain types of crime. This practice is known as racial profiling. Do you approve or disapprove of the use of racial profiling by police?
  - NPR/Harvard/Kaiser Family Foundation, October 2001 and 2005

Hate crime law:

- I'm going to mention several different proposals that have been made recently. For each one, please tell me whether you strongly favor, somewhat favor, somewhat oppose, or strongly oppose that proposal. Imposing a tougher sentence for someone who commits a so-called "hate crime" in which they specifically target their victim as a member of a minority group than for someone who otherwise commits the same crime.
  - Kiley & Company, October 1998
- Some states have special laws that provide harsher penalties for crimes motivated by hate of certain groups than the same penalties for the same crimes if they are not motivated by this kind of hate. Would you favor or oppose this type of hate crime law in your state?
  - Gallup Poll, February 1999
- How do you feel about "hate crime" laws that impose extra penalties on those who assault someone on account of the victim's race, religion, ethnic group, or sexual preference? Do you think that extra penalties for this type of crime are a good idea or a bad idea?
  - Carolina Poll, 1999

Hate crime law covering sexual orientation:

- Do you favor or oppose a federal law that would impose additional penalties on people who commit crimes out of prejudice toward gays and lesbians?
  - *Washington Post*/Kaiser Family Foundation/Harvard University, September 2000

NOTES

1 Direct Democracy Institutions and the Threat of Tyranny

1 J. W. Sullivan, 1893. *Direct Legislation by the Citizenship through the Initiative and Referendum*. New York: True Nationalist Publishing.
2 For example, Henry Steele Commager, 1958. *Majority Rule and Minority Rights, The James W. Richards Lectures in History*. Gloucester, MA: Peter Smith.
3 For example, Barbara S. Gamble, 1997. "Putting Civil Rights to a Popular Vote." *American Journal of Political Science* 41 (1):245–69; and Zoltan L. Hajnal, Elisabeth R. Gerber, and Hugh Louch, 2002. "Minorities and Direct Legislation: Evidence from California Ballot Proposition Elections." *Journal of Politics* 64 (1):154–77.
4 John G. Matsusaka, 2004. *For the Many or the Few: The Initiative, Public Policy, and American Democracy, American Politics and Political Economy*. Chicago, IL: University of Chicago Press, p. 117.
5 For example, James Madison, [1787] 1999. "No. 10: The Same Subject Continued." In *The Federalist Papers*, ed. A. Hamilton, J. Madison, and J. Jay. New York: Penguin Books.
6 Thomas E. Cronin, 1989. *Direct Democracy: The Politics of Initiative, Referendum, and Recall*. Cambridge, MA: Harvard University Press.
7 John Haskell, 2001. *Direct Democracy or Representative Government?: Dispelling the Populist Myth*. Boulder, CO: Westview Press.
8 David D. Schmidt, 1989. *Citizen Lawmakers: The Ballot Initiative Revolution*. Philadelphia, PA: Temple University Press.
9 Nathan Cree, 1892. *Direct Legislation by the People*. Chicago, IL: A. C. McClurg, p. 16.
10 Cronin, *Direct Democracy: The Politics of Initiative, Referendum, and Recall*.
11 Daniel A. Smith and Dustin Fridkin, 2008. "Delegating Direct Democracy: Interparty Legislative Competition and the Adoption of the Initiative in the American States." *American Political Science Review* 102 (3):333–50.
12 Matsusaka, *For the Many or the Few: The Initiative, Public Policy, and American Democracy, American Politics and Political Economy*.

13   For example, Arthur Lupia, Yanna Krupnikov, Adam Seth Levine, Spencer Piston, and Alexander Von Hagen-Jamar. 2010. "Why State Constitutions Differ in their Treatment of Same-Sex Marriage." *Journal of Politics* 72 (4):1222–35.

14   Shaun Bowler and Todd Donovan, 2004. "Measuring the Effects of Direct Democracy on State Policy: Not all Initiatives are Created Equal." *State Politics and Policy Quarterly* 4:345–63.

15   For example, Ronald E. Weber and Paul Brace, eds, 1999. *American State and Local Politics: Directions for the 21st Century*. New York: Chatham House; and Christopher Z. Mooney, 2001. "State Politics and Policy Quarterly and the Study of State Politics: The Editor's Introduction." *State Politics and Policy Quarterly* 1 (1):1–4.

16   Shaun Bowler and Todd Donovan. 2008. "The Initiative Process." In *Politics in the American States, a Comparative Analysis*, ed. V. and R. L. Hanson Gray. Washington, DC: CQ Press; and Caroline J. Tolbert, John Grummel, and Daniel Smith, 2001. "The Effects of Ballot Initiatives on Voter Turnout in the United States." *American Politics Research* 29 (6):625–48.

17   John G. Matsusaka, 1995. "Fiscal Effects of the Voter Initiative: Evidence from the Last 30 Years." *Journal of Political Economy* 103 (3):587–623; Shaun Bowler, Todd Donovan, and Caroline Tolbert, 1998. *Citizens as Legislators: Direct Democracy in the United States*. Columbus: Ohio State University Press; John G. Matsusaka and Nolan M. McCarty, 2001. "Political Resource Allocation: Benefits and Costs of Voter Initiatives." *Journal of Law Economics & Organization* 17 (2):413–48; and Kevin Arceneaux, 2002. "Direct Democracy and the Link between Public Opinion and State Abortion Policy." *State Politics and Policy Quarterly* 2 (4):372–87.

18   Matsusaka, *For the Many or the Few: The Initiative, Public Policy, and American Democracy*, *American Politics and Political Economy*.

19   Elisabeth R. Gerber, 1996. "Legislative Response to the Threat of Popular Initiatives." *American Journal of Political Science* 40 (1):99–128; Elisabeth R. Gerber, 1999. *The Populist Paradox: Interest Group Influence and the Promise of Direct Legislation*. Princeton, NJ: Princeton University Press; Matsusaka and McCarty, "Political Resource Allocation: Benefits and Costs of Voter Initiatives"; and Barry C. Burden, 2005. "Institutions and Policy Representation in the States." *State Politics and Policy Quarterly* 5 (4):373–93.

20   Cronin, *Direct Democracy: The Politics of Initiative, Referendum, and Recall*.

21   James Madison, [1787] 1999. "No. 51: The Structure of Government Must Furnish the Proper Checks and Balances between the Different Departments." In *The Federalist Papers*, ed. A. Hamilton, J. Madison, and J. Jay. New York: Penguin Putnam, p. 291.

22   Madison, "No. 10: The Same Subject Continued," p. 50.

23   For example, Gary W. Cox and Mathew D. McCubbins, 2007. *Legislative Leviathan: Party Government in the House*. 2nd ed. Cambridge, New York: Cambridge University Press.

24   Bruce E. Cain and Kenneth P. Miller, 2001. "The Populist Legacy: Initiatives and the Undermining of Representative Government." In *Dangerous Democracy? The Battle Over Ballot Initiatives in America*, ed. L. J. Sabato, H. R. Ernst, and B. A. Larson. Lanham, MD: Rowman & Littlefield Publishers, Inc.; and Derrick Bell, 1978. "The Referendum: Democracy's Barrier to Racial Equality." *Washington Law Review* 54:1–29.

25   Frederick J. Boehmke, 2002. "The Effect of Direct Democracy on the Size and Diversity of State Interest Group Populations." *Journal of Politics* 64 (3):827–44; Daniel A. Smith and Caroline J. Tolbert, 2004. *Educated by Initiative: The Effects of Direct Democracy on Citizens and Political Organizations in the American States*. Ann Arbor, MI: University of Michigan Press; and Frederick J. Boehmke, 2005. "Sources of Variation

in the Frequency of Statewide Initiatives: The Role of Interest Group Populations." *Political Research Quarterly* 58 (4):565–75.

26 Gerber, *The Populist Paradox: Interest Group Influence and the Promise of Direct Legislation.*

27 Julian N. Eule, 1990. "Judicial Review of Direct Democracy." *Yale Law Journal* 99 (7):1503–90; and Cain and Miller, "The Populist Legacy: Initiatives and the Undermining of Representative Government."

28 E. E. Schattschneider, 1960. *The Semisovereign People; a Realist's View of Democracy in America.* 1st ed. New York: Holt; and Donald P. Haider-Markel and Kenneth J. Meier, 1996. "The Politics of Gay and Lesbian Rights: Expanding the Scope of the Conflict." *Journal of Politics* 58 (2):332–49.

29 Thomas Romer and Howard Rosenthal, 1979. "The Elusive Median Voter." *Journal of Public Economics* 12 (2):143–70; and Gerber, "Legislative Response to the Threat of Popular Initiatives."

30 For example, Kenneth J. Meier, 1975. "Representative Bureaucracy: An Empirical Analysis." *American Political Science Review* 69 (2):526–42; and Kenneth J. Meier, 1993. "Latinos and Representative Bureaucracy Testing the Thompson and Henderson Hypotheses." *Journal of Public Administration Research and Theory: J-PART* 3 (4):393–414.

31 Gerber, *The Populist Paradox: Interest Group Influence and the Promise of Direct Legislation*; and Gerber, "Legislative Response to the Threat of Popular Initiatives."

32 Elisabeth R. Gerber and Simon Hug, 2001. "Legislative Responses to Referendum." In *Referendum Democracy: Citizens, Elites, and Deliberation in Referendum Campaigns*, ed. M. Mendelsohn and A. Parkin. Toronto: Macmillan/St Martin's Press.

33 Clayton P. Gillette, 1988. "Plebiscites, Participation, and Collective Action in Local Government Law." *Michigan Law Review* 86 (5):930–88.

34 Richard Ellis, 2002. *Democratic Delusions: The Initiative Process in America.* Lawrence: University Press of Kansas.

35 Eule, "Judicial Review of Direct Democracy."

36 Mads Qvortrup, 2001. "The Courts vs. the People: An Essay on Judicial Review of Initiatives." In *The Battle over Citizen Law Making*, ed. M. D. Waters. Durham, NC: Carolina Academic Press; and Kenneth P. Miller, 2009. *Direct Democracy and the Courts.* New York: Cambridge University Press.

37 Joseph R. Grodin, 1988. "Developing a Consensus of Restraint: A Judge's Perspective on Judicial Retention Elections." *Southern California Law Review* 61:1961.

38 Daniel C. Lewis and Frederick S. Wood, 2009. "Direct Democracy, Minority Rights, and Judicial Review." Paper read at the Annual Meeting of the Midwest Political Science Association, April 2–5, at Chicago, IL.

39 Mathew Manweller, 2005. "The Angriest Crocodile: Information Costs, Direct Democracy Activists, and the Politicization of State Judicial Elections." *State and Local Government Review* 37 (2):86–102.

40 Miki Caul Kittilson and Katherine Tate, 2005. "Political Parties, Minorities, and Elected Office." In *The Politics of Democratic Inclusion*, ed. R. E. Hero and C. Wolbrecht. Philadelphia, PA: Temple University Press, p. 182.

41 Hajnal, Gerber, and Louch, "Minorities and Direct Legislation: Evidence from California Ballot Proposition Elections."

42 It is also these policies that have been the focus of previous scholarly examinations of this question. So in order to speak directly to this line of research, it is important to assess similar issues. A full discussion of the existing literature follows in the succeeding section.

43 Donald P. Haider-Markel, Alana Querze, and Kara Lindaman, 2007. "Lose, Win, or Draw? A Reexamination of Direct Democracy and Minority Rights." *Political Research Quarterly* 60 (2):304–14.

44 David B. Magleby, 1984. *Direct Legislation: Voting on Ballot Propositions in the United States*. Baltimore, MD: Johns Hopkins University Press; and Cronin, *Direct Democracy: The Politics of Initiative, Referendum, and Recall*.

45 Donovan and Bowler, "Direct Democracy and Minority Rights: An Extension"; and Todd Donovan and Shaun Bowler, 1998. "Responsive or Responsible Government." In *Citizens as Legislators*, ed. S. Bowler, T. Donovan, and C. J. Tolbert. Columbus, OH: Ohio State University Press.

46 Hajnal, Gerber, and Louch, "Minorities and Direct Legislation: Evidence from California Ballot Proposition Elections."

47 Bruno S. Frey and Lorenz Goette, 1998. "Does the Popular Vote Destroy Civil Rights?" *American Journal of Political Science* 42 (4):1343–8.

48 Gamble, "Putting Civil Rights to a Popular Vote."

49 However, Donovan and Bowler demonstrate that these passage rates may not be accurate given the non-representative sample used in Gamble's study. See Donovan and Bowler, "Direct Democracy and Minority Rights: An Extension."

50 Examples of studies of Official English include Raymond Tatalovich, 1995. *Nativism Reborn?: The Official English Language Movement and the American States*. Lexington, KY: University Press of Kentucky; Deborah, J. Schildkraut, 2001. "Official-English and the States: Influences on Declaring English the Official Language in the United States." *Political Research Quarterly* 54 (2):445–57; and Robert R. Preuhs, 2005. "Descriptive Representation, Legislative Leadership, and Direct Democracy: Latino Influence on English Only Laws in the States, 1984–2002." *State Politics and Policy Quarterly* 5 (3):203–24. For an example of a study on affirmative action bans, see Lydia Chávez, 1998. *The Color Bind: California's Battle to End Affirmative Action*. Berkeley: University of California Press. Anti-gay rights policies were studied in Haider-Markel, Querze, and Lindaman, "Lose, Win, or Draw? A Reexamination of Direct Democracy and Minority Rights."

51 Gerber and Hug, "Legislative Responses to Referendum."

52 Madison, "No. 10: The Same Subject Continued."

53 Schildkraut, "Official-English and the States: Influences on Declaring English the Official Language in the United States"; and Preuhs, "Descriptive Representation, Legislative Leadership, and Direct Democracy: Latino Influence on English Only Laws in the States, 1984–2002."

2 Direct Democracy and the Diffusion of Anti-Minority Policies

1 For a more detailed exploration of this issue, see Daniel R. Pinello, 2006. *America's Struggle for Same-Sex Marriage*. New York: Cambridge University Press.

2 For example, Minnesota Supreme Court in 1971, Arizona Supreme Court in 1975— for more detailed information, see Rachel Kranz and Tim Cusick, 2005. *Gay Rights*. Rev. ed. Library in a Book. New York, NY: Facts on File.

3 The timeline shows each state's initial adoption, not subsequent constitutional amendments, because it is the initial adoption that serves to change the *status quo* policy and restrict the rights of homosexuals. Constitutional amendments passed afterward reinforced the existing policy and made it more difficult to overturn, but did not substantively change those states' policies toward same-sex marriage.

4   For example, Jack L. Walker, 1969. "The Diffusion of Innovations among the American States." *American Political Science Review* 63 (3):880–99.

5   For example, Frances Stokes Berry and William D. Berry, 1990. "State Lottery Adoptions as Policy Innovations: An Event History Analysis." *American Political Science Review* 84 (2):395–415; and Virginia Gray, 1973. "Innovation in the States: A Diffusion Study." *American Political Science Review* 67 (4):1174–85.

6   Two of these ballot measures were considered during primary elections rather than the general elections. For a further discussion of the 2004 elections and same-sex marriage ballot measures, see Todd Donovan, Caroline J. Tolbert, and Daniel A. Smith, 2008. "Priming Presidential Votes by Direct Democracy." *Journal of Politics* 70:1217–31.

7   For an in-depth look at how the institutional design of the constitutional amendment process affected same-sex marriage policy in the states, see Lupia, Krupnikov, and Levine, "Why State Constitutions Differ in their Treatment of Same-Sex Marriage."

8   Due to data limitations, the analyses end in 2006. Nebraska is excluded from the analysis because of its nonpartisan legislature.

9   For more information on this model and many other event history models, see Janet M. Box-Steffensmeier and Bradford S. Jones, 2004. *Event History Modeling: A Guide for Social Scientists*. New York: Cambridge University Press.

10   Shaun Bowler and Todd Donovan, 2004. "Measuring the Effects of Direct Democracy on State Policy: Not All Initiatives are Created Equal." *State Politics and Policy Quarterly* 4:345–63.

11   John Pippen, Shaun Bowler, and Todd Donovan. 2002. "Election Reform and Direct Democracy: Campaign Finance Regulations in the American States." *American Politics Research* 30 (6):559–82.

12   Bowler and Donovan, "Measuring the Effects of Direct Democracy on State Policy: Not all Initiatives are Created Equal."

13   The original scoring based on the PCA creates a measure with a mean of zero. I adjusted the measure for easier substantive interpretation, so that non-direct democracy states would have a score of zero, rather than a negative score.

14   William D. Berry, Evan J. Ringquist, Richard C. Fording, and Russell L. Hanson, 1998. "Measuring Citizen and Government Ideology in the American States, 1960–93." *American Journal of Political Science* 42 (1): 327–48; and William D. Berry, Evan J. Ringquist, Richard C. Fording, and Russell L. Hanson, 2007. "1960–2006 Citizen Ideology Series." ICPSR. I opt for this measure rather than the survey-based ideology scores developed in Robert S. Erikson, Gerald C. Wright, and John P. McIver, 1993. *Statehouse Democracy: Public Opinion and Policy in the American States*. Cambridge: Cambridge University Press because of the latter's exclusion of both Hawaii and Alaska. Alternative specifications that use the Erickson, Wright, and McIver measure of ideology show no appreciable differences.

15   Ideally, the analyses would also include public attitudes toward same-sex marriage, but, unfortunately, dynamic state-level issue attitudes have yet to be developed. This issue is discussed in more detail in Chapter 5. Including a static measure of support for same-sex marriage from 2008 does not substantively change the results of the analyses.

16   Kenneth D. Wald, James W. Button, and Barbara A. Rienzo, 1996. "The Politics of Gay Rights in American Communities: Explaining Antidiscrimination Ordinances and Policies." *American Journal of Political Science* 40 (4):1152–78; and Donald P. Haider-Markel, 2001. "Policy Diffusion as a Geographic Expansion of the Scope of Political Conflict: Same-Sex Marriage Bans in the 1990s." *State Politics and Policy Quarterly* 1 (1):2–26.

17 Association of Statisticians of American Religious Bodies, 2002. "Religious Congregations and Membership Study, 2000." Glenmary Research Center.

18 Simple counts of self-identified homosexuals in the states tend to underestimate the gay population. One study estimates that the 2000 Census undercounted the gay population by 62 percent: David M. Smith and Gary J. Gates, 2001. "Gay and Lesbian Families in the United States: Same-Sex Unmarried Partner Households." Washington, DC: Human Rights Campaign.

19 Austin Ranney, 1976. "Parties in State Politics." In *Politics in the American States: A Comparative Analysis*, ed. H. Jacob and K. N. Vines. Boston, MA: Little, Brown.

20 For example, Robert L. Crain, 1966. "Fluoridation: The Diffusion of an Innovation among Cities." *Social Forces* 44 (4):467–76; James M. Lutz, 1986. "The Spatial and Temporal Diffusion of Selected Licensing Laws in the United States." *Political Geography Quarterly* 5:141–59; and Berry and Berry "State Lottery Adoptions as Policy Innovations: An Event History Analysis.

21 Alternative specifications that do not include these legal environment variables produce substantively similar results.

22 Following the *Lawrence v. Texas* decision in 2003, all sodomy laws were struck down.

23 *WISC. STAT. §765.001(2).*

24 Donovan and Bowler, "Direct Democracy and Minority Rights: An Extension." But also see Haider-Markel, Querze, and Lindaman, "Lose, Win, or Draw? A Re-examination of Direct Democracy and Minority Rights."

25 For example, Herbert McClosky and Alida Brill, 1983. *Dimensions of Tolerance: What Americans Believe about Civil Liberties.* New York: Russell Sage Foundation.

26 Gregory M. Herek and John P. Capitanio, 1995. "Black Heterosexuals' Attitudes toward Lesbians and Gay Men in the United States." *Journal of Sex Research* 32 (2):95–105; and Stephanie Slade and Daniel A. Smith, 2011. "Obama to Blame? Minority Surge Voters and the Ban on Same-Sex Marriage in Florida." *The Forum* 9 (2).

27 Clyde Wilcox and Robin Wolpert, 2000. "Gay Rights in the Public Sphere: Public Opinion on Gay and Lesbian Equality." In *The Politics of Gay Rights*, ed. W. Rimmerman and Clyde Wilcox. Chicago, IL: University of Chicago Press.

28 Dennis E. Baron, 1990. *The English-Only Question: An Official Language for Americans?* New Haven, CT: Yale University Press.

29 Carol L. Schmid, 2001. *The Politics of Language: Conflict, Identity and Cultural Pluralism in a Comparative Perspective.* New York: Oxford University Press.

30 Heinz Kloss, 1977. *The American Bilingual Tradition.* Rowley, MA: Newbury House.

31 James Crawford, 1992. *Language Loyalties: A Source Book on the Official English Controversy.* Chicago: University of Chicago Press.

32 Ronald Schmidt, 2000. *Language Policy and Identity Politics in the United States.* Philadelphia, PA: Temple University Press.

33 Ibid.

34 The amendment originally declared "American" as the official language, reflecting the broad nativist attitudes of the time, but in the end English was chosen to avoid confusion. See, Tatalovich, *Nativism Reborn?: The Official English Language Movement and the American States.*

35 Ibid.

36 Louisiana, Nebraska, Illinois, Massachusetts, and Hawaii are excluded from the analysis because they all adopted an official language policy prior to the contemporary English Only movement.

37 Tatalovich, *Nativism Reborn?: The Official English Language Movement and the American States*.

38 V. O. Key, 1949. *Southern Politics in State and Nation*. New York: Vintage Books; Hubert M. Blalock, 1967. *Toward a Theory of Minority-Group Relations*. New York: Wiley; Caroline J. Tolbert and Rodney E. Hero, 1996. "Race/Ethnicity and Direct Democracy: An Analysis of California's Illegal Immigration Initiative." *Journal of Politics* 58 (3):806–18; Caroline J. Tolbert and John A. Grummel, 2003. "Revisiting the Racial Threat Hypothesis: White Voter Support for California's Proposition 209." *State Politics and Policy Quarterly* 3 (2):183.

39 Tatalovich, *Nativism Reborn?: The Official English Language Movement and the American States*; and Tolbert and Grummel, "Revisiting the Racial Threat Hypothesis: White Voter Support for California's Proposition 209."

40 Schildkraut, "Official-English and the States: Influences on Declaring English the Official Language in the United States."

41 Ibid.; Preuhs, "Descriptive Representation, Legislative Leadership, and Direct Democracy: Latino Influence on English Only Laws in the States, 1984–2002."

42 The foreign-born population data is available from the U.S. Census Bureau for 1980, 1990, and from 1994 to 2007. Data between 1980 and 1990, and between 1990 and 1994, are interpolated.

43 Schildkraut, "Official-English and the States: Influences on Declaring English the Official Language in the United States."

44 Following the analyses of Schildkraut and Preuhs I include a dichotomous indicator for Southern states. Omitting this variable from this analysis does not substantively change the results. Similarly, including this variable in the other analyses presented here does not substantively affect the results.

45 Figure 2.6 shows the hazards rates only for 1994 (the midpoint of the dataset), but other years display similar patterns.

46 Tatalovich, *Nativism Reborn?: The Official English Language Movement and the American States*.

47 Sean Nicholson-Crotty, 2006. "Reassessing Madison's Diversity Hypothesis: The Case of Same-Sex Marriage." *Journal of Politics* 68 (4):922–30.

48 John Fobanjong, 2001. *Understanding the Backlash against Affirmative Action*. Huntington, NY: Nova Science Publishers.

49 Peter Shrag, 2001. "An Alligator in the Bathtub: Assessing Initiative Reform Proposals." In *Dangerous Democracy? The Battle over Ballot Initiatives in America*, ed. Larry J. Sabato, Howard R. Ernst, and Bruce A. Larson. Lanham, MD: Rowman & Littlefield Publishers, Inc.

50 For a more detailed account of the history of affirmative action in the United States, see Terry H. Anderson, 2004. *The Pursuit of Fairness: A History of Affirmative Action*. New York: Oxford University Press.

51 Rodney E. Hero and Caroline J. Tolbert, 1996. "A Racial/Ethnic Diversity Interpretation of Politics and Policy in the States of the U.S." *American Journal of Political Science* 40 (3):851–71.

52 California was the second most diverse state in the country in the 2000 Census, as measured by the minority diversity index. Michigan, Washington, and Nebraska ranked 24th, 25th, and 38th respectively.

53 Anderson, *The Pursuit of Fairness: A History of Affirmative Action*.

54 Oscar Eason Jr., 1998. "Retrospective on Campaign for Initiative 200." *Seattle Post-Intelligencer*, November 12, 1998, A15; Tamar Lewin, 2006. "Michigan Rejects Affirmative Action, and Backers Sue." *New York Times*, November 9, 2006.

55   William March, 1999. "Bush Readies Affirmative-Action Policies under Mounting Pressure." *Tampa Tribune*, November 7, 1999, 1.

56   The case made further headlines in 1997 when a civil rights coalition dropped their appeal to the Supreme Court, fearing that another decision like *Hopwood v. Texas* would further erode affirmative action programs in the United States.

57   Anderson, *The Pursuit of Fairness: A History of Affirmative Action*.

58   www.ncsl.org/legislatures-elections/legisdata/african-american-legislators-2003.aspx; www.ncsl.org/legislatures-elections/legisdata/latino-legislators-2003.aspx.

3   A Representational Filter? The Passage of Anti-Minority Policy Proposals

1   Keyword searches were conducted through Lexis Nexis State Capital, the National Conference of State Legislature's Ballot Measure Database, and individual state legislative bill archives. The following search terms were used: "homosexual," "gay," "same-sex," "civil union," "marriage," "English language," "Official English," "English education," "affirmative action," "racial preferences," "discriminate," and "civil rights."

2   *P* values less than 0.05 are considered to be statistically significant.

3   Tatalovich, *Nativism Reborn?: The Official English Language Movement and the American States*; Schildkraut, "Official-English and the States: Influences on Declaring English the Official Language in the United States"; and Preuhs, "Descriptive Representation, Legislative Leadership, and Direct Democracy: Latino Influence on English Only Laws in the States, 1984–2002."

4   Ranney, "Parties in State Politics."

5   Legislative professsionalization is measured with the Squire Index; Peverill Squire, 1992. "Legislative Professionalization and Membership Diversity in State Legislatures." *Legislative Studies Quarterly* 17 (1):69–79. Peverill Squire, 2000. "Uncontested Seats in State Legislative Elections." *Legislative Studies Quarterly* 25 (1): 131–46; and Peverill Squire, 2007. "Measuring State Legislative Professionalism: The Squire Index Revisited." *State Politics and Policy Quarterly* 7 (2):211–27.

6   An alternative specification, using the Erikson, McIver, and Wright measure of public ideology was also utilized, producing very similar results. William D. Berry, Evan J. Ringquist, Richard C. Fording, and Russell L. Hanson, 2007. "1960–2006 Citizen Ideology Series." ICPSR.

7   Rodney E. Hero, 1998. *Faces of Inequality: Social Diversity in American Politics*. New York: Oxford University Press.

8   For example, see McCloskey and Brill, *Dimensions of Tolerance: What Americans Believe about Civil Liberties*.

9   Tatalovich, *Nativism Reborn?: The Official English Language Movement and the American States*.

10   Alexander Hamilton, James Madison, and John Jay. [1787] 1999. *The Federalist Papers*, ed. C. Rossiter. New York: Penguin Books.

11   Alternative determinants of proposal passage that were considered but not presented here include political culture, income per capita, and region. These variables do not add any additional explanatory power to the models and excluding them does not alter the interpretation of the direct democracy coefficients.

12   Alternative goodness-of-fit measures, like other pseudo R2 statistics, the Hosmer-Lemeshow χ^2 and the proportional reduction in error λ, all suggest that the models fit the data well and are improvements over the null prediction of the modal category (not pass).

13 Peverill Squire and Keith E. Hamm, 2005. *101 Chambers: Congress, State Legislatures, and the Future of Legislative Studies.* Columbus, OH: Ohio State University Press.

4 The Flip Side; Direct Democracy and Pro-Minority Policies

1 Gamble, "Putting Civil Rights to a Popular Vote"; Donovan and Bowler, "Direct Democracy and Minority Rights: An Extension"; and Haider-Markel, Querze, and Lindaman, "Lose, Win, or Draw? A Reexamination of Direct Democracy and Minority Rights."

2 Haider-Markel, Querze, and Lindaman, "Lose, Win, or Draw? A Reexamination of Direct Democracy and Minority Rights."

3 This study focuses on broad nondiscrimination policies that extend across most of these components. However, recent work highlights the differences in the policy process across these various components; see Jami K. Taylor, Daniel C. Lewis, Matthew L. Jacobsmeier, and Brian DiSarro, "Content and Complexity in Policy Reinvention and Diffusion." *State Politics and Policy Quarterly* 12 (1):75–98.

4 This study only examines nondiscrimination policies as they pertain to sexual orientation inclusiveness. For work on gender identity protections, see Taylor, Lewis, Jacobsmeier, and DiSarro, "Content and Complexity in Policy Reinvention and Diffusion."

5 James W. Button, Barbara Ann Rienzo, and Kenneth D. Wald, 1997. *Private Lives, Public Conflicts: Battles over Gay Rights in American Communities.* Washington, DC: CQ Press.

6 Nebraska is excluded because of its nonpartisan legislature. Models that include Nebraska and are estimated without party variables do not significantly change the results regarding the effect of direct democracy.

7 Political culture, racial diversity, legislative professionalization, per capita income, and region were included in alternate models but they added no significant explanatory power to the models and are not presented here.

8 The variable indicating unified Republican government is not included in the models because it perfectly predicts failure to adopt the policy and estimates of the standard error cannot be estimated.

9 A full discussion of these control variables is included in Chapter 2.

10 ACLU. 2007. *Racial Profiling: Definition* 2005 [cited June 2007]. Available from www.aclu.org/racialjustice/racialprofiling/21741res20051123.html.

11 Racial Profiling Data Collection Resource Center, 2007. *History of Racial Profiling Analysis* 2007 [cited June 2007]. Available from www.racialprofilinganalysis.neu.edu/background/history.php.

12 Nebraska is excluded because of its nonpartisan legislature. Models that include Nebraska and are estimated without party variables do not significantly change the results regarding the effect of direct democracy.

13 Again, political culture, racial diversity, legislative professionalization, per capita income, and region were included in alternate models for all of the analyses in this chapter, but added no significant explanatory power to the models and are not presented here.

14 Hero, *Faces of Inequality: Social Diversity in American Politics.*

15 Madison, "No. 10: The Same Subject Continued."

16 Fred C. Pampel, 2004. *Racial Profiling.* New York: Facts on File.

17 *Hate Crime Statistics Act.* Public Law No.101–275. April 23, 1990.

18   Donald Altschiller, 2005. *Hate Crimes: A Reference Handbook*. 2nd ed. Santa Barbara, CA: ABC-CLIO.

19   Valerie Jenness and Ryken Grattet, 2001. *Making Hate a Crime: From Social Movement to Law Enforcement*. New York: Russell Sage Foundation.

20   Nebraska is excluded because of its nonpartisan legislature. Models that include Nebraska and are estimated without party variables do not significantly change the results regarding the effect of direct democracy.

21   For example, Donald P. Haider-Markel, 1998. "The Politics of Social Regulatory Policy: State and Federal Hate Crime Policy and Implementation Effort." *Political Research Quarterly* 51 (1):69–88; and Mahalley D. Allen, Carrie Pettus, and Donald P. Haider-Markel, 2004. "Making the National Local: Specifying the Conditions for National Government Influence on State Policymaking." *State Politics and Policy Quarterly* 4 (3):318–44.

22   Bureau of Justice Statistics, 1994. "Hate Crimes Reported in NIBRS, 1990–1992," ed. U. S. D. o. Justice; and Bureau of Justice Statistics, 2001. "Hate Crimes Reported in NIBRS, 1997–1999," ed. U. S. D. o. Justice.

23   Nebraska is excluded from the analysis because of its nonpartisan legislature. Models that include Nebraska and are estimated without party variables do not significantly change the results regarding the effect of direct democracy.

5 Conclusion

1   Tatalovich, *Nativism Reborn?: The Official English Language Movement and the American States*; Schildkraut, "Official-English and the States: Influences on Declaring English the Official Language in the United States"; and Preuhs, "Descriptive Representation, Legislative Leadership, and Direct Democracy: Latino Influence on English Only Laws in the States, 1984–2002."

2   Madison, "No. 51: The Structure of Government Must Furnish the Proper Checks and Balances Between the Different Departments." p. 291.

3   For example, Erikson, Wright, and McIver, *Statehouse Democracy: Public Opinion and Policy in the American States*; and Berry, Ringquist, Fording, and Hanson, "Measuring Citizen and Government Ideology in the American States, 1960–93."

4   Jeffrey R. Lax and Justin H. Phillips, 2009. "How Should We Estimate Public Opinion in the States?" *American Journal of Political Science* 53 (1):107–21; and Jeffrey R. Lax and Justin H. Phillips, 2009. "Gay Rights in the States: Public Opinion and Policy Responsiveness." *American Political Science Review* 103 (03):367–86.

5   Specific citations and question wordings are present in the Appendix.

6   Ibid.

7   Frey and Goette, "Does the Popular Vote Destroy Civil Rights?"

BIBLIOGRAPHY

ACLU. "Racial Profiling: Definition." www.aclu.org/racialjustice/racialprofiling/21741 res20051123.html.

Allen, Mahalley D., Carrie Pettus, and Donald P. Haider-Markel. 2004. "Making the National Local: Specifying the Conditions for National Government Influence on State Policymaking." *State Politics and Policy Quarterly* 4, no. 3: 318–44.

Altschiller, Donald. 2005. *Hate Crimes: A Reference Handbook*. 2nd ed, Contemporary World Issues. Santa Barbara, CA: ABC-CLIO.

Anderson, Terry H. 2004. *The Pursuit of Fairness: A History of Affirmative Action*. New York: Oxford University Press.

Arceneaux, Kevin. 2002. "Direct Democracy and the Link between Public Opinion and State Abortion Policy." *State Politics and Policy Quarterly* 2, no. 4: 372–87.

Association of Statisticians of American Religious Bodies. 2002. "Religious Congregations and Membership Study, 2000." Glenmary Research Center.

Baron, Dennis E. 1990. *The English-Only Question: An Official Language for Americans?* New Haven, CT: Yale University Press.

Bell, Derrick. 1978. "The Referendum: Democracy's Barrier to Racial Equality." *Washington Law Review* 54: 1–29.

Berry, Frances Stokes, and William D. Berry. 1990. "State Lottery Adoptions as Policy Innovations: An Event History Analysis." *American Political Science Review* 84, no. 2: 395–415.

Berry, William D., Evan J. Ringquist, Richard C. Fording, and Russell L. Hanson. 1998. "Measuring Citizen and Government Ideology in the American States, 1960–93." *American Journal of Political Science* 42, no. 1: 327–48.

Berry, William D., Evan J. Ringquist, Richard C. Fording, and Russell L. Hanson. 2003. "1960–2002 Citizen Ideology Series." ICPSR.

Berry, William D., Evan J. Ringquist, Richard C. Fording, and Russell L. Hanson. 2007. "1960–2006 Citizen Ideology Series." ICPSR.

Blalock, Hubert M. 1967. *Toward a Theory of Minority-Group Relations*. New York: Wiley.

Boehmke, Frederick J. 2002. "The Effect of Direct Democracy on the Size and Diversity of State Interest Group Populations." *Journal of Politics* 64, no. 3: 827–44.

Boehmke, Frederick J. 2005. "Sources of Variation in the Frequency of Statewide Initiatives: The Role of Interest Group Populations." *Political Research Quarterly* 58, no. 4: 565–75.

Bowler, Shaun, and Todd Donovan. 2004. "Measuring the Effects of Direct Democracy on State Policy: Not All Initiatives Are Created Equal." *State Politics and Policy Quarterly* 4: 345–63.

Bowler, Shaun, and Todd Donovan. 2008. "The Initiative Process." In *Politics in the American States, a Comparative Analysis*, edited by Virginia and Russell L. Hanson Gray. Washington, DC: CQ Press.

Bowler, Shaun, Todd Donovan, and Caroline Tolbert. 1998. *Citizens as Legislators: Direct Democracy in the United States*, Parliaments and Legislatures Series. Columbus, OH: Ohio State University Press.

Box-Steffensmeier, Janet M., and Bradford S. Jones. 2004. *Event History Modeling: A Guide for Social Scientists*. Cambridge; New York: Cambridge University Press.

Burden, Barry C. 2005. "Institutions and Policy Representation in the States." *State Politics and Policy Quarterly* 5, no. 4: 373–93.

Button, James W., Barbara Ann Rienzo, and Kenneth D. Wald. 1997. *Private Lives, Public Conflicts: Battles over Gay Rights in American Communities*. Washington, DC: CQ Press.

Cain, Bruce E., and Kenneth P. Miller. 2001. "The Populist Legacy: Initiatives and the Undermining of Representative Government." In *Dangerous Democracy? The Battle over Ballot Initiatives in America*, edited by Larry J. Sabato, Howard R. Ernst, and Bruce A. Larson. Lanham, MD: Rowman & Littlefield Publishers, Inc.

Center, Racial Profiling Data Collection Resource. "History of Racial Profiling Analysis." www.racialprofilinganalysis.neu.edu/background/history.php.

Chávez, Lydia. 1998. *The Color Bind: California's Battle to End Affirmative Action*. Berkeley, CA: University of California Press.

Commager, Henry Steele. 1958. *Majority Rule and Minority Rights*, The James W. Richards Lectures in History. Gloucester, MA: Peter Smith.

Cox, Gary W., and Mathew D. McCubbins. 2007. *Legislative Leviathan: Party Government in the House*. 2nd ed. Cambridge; New York: Cambridge University Press.

Crain, Robert L. 1966. "Fluoridation: The Diffusion of an Innovation among Cities." *Social Forces* 44, no. 4: 467–76.

Crawford, James. 1992. *Language Loyalties: A Source Book on the Official English Controversy*. Chicago, IL: University of Chicago Press.

Cree, Nathan. 1892. *Direct Legislation by the People*. Chicago, IL: A.C. McClurg.

Cronin, Thomas E. 1989. *Direct Democracy: The Politics of Initiative, Referendum, and Recall*. Cambridge, MA: Harvard University Press.

Donovan, Todd, and Shaun Bowler. 1998. "Direct Democracy and Minority Rights: An Extension." *American Journal of Political Science* 42, no. 3: 1020–4.

Donovan, Todd, and Shaun Bowler. 1998. "Responsive or Responsible Government." In *Citizens as Legislators*, edited by Shaun Bowler, Todd Donovan, and Caroline J. Tolbert. Columbus, OH: Ohio State University Press.

Donovan, Todd, Caroline J. Tolbert, and Daniel A. Smith. 2008. "Priming Presidential Votes by Direct Democracy." *Journal of Politics* 70: 1217–31.

Eason Jr., Oscar. 1998. "Retrospective on Campaign for Initiative 200." *Seattle Post-Intelligencer*, November 12, 1998, A15.

Ellis, Richard. 2002. *Democratic Delusions: The Initiative Process in America*, Studies in Government and Public Policy. Lawrence, KS: University Press of Kansas.

Erikson, Robert S., Gerald C. Wright, and John P. McIver. 1993. *Statehouse Democracy: Public Opinion and Policy in the American States.* Cambridge: Cambridge University Press.

Eule, Julian N. 1990. "Judicial Review of Direct Democracy." *Yale Law Journal* 99, no. 7: 1503–90.

Fobanjong, John. 2001. *Understanding the Backlash against Affirmative Action.* Huntington, NY: Nova Science Publishers.

Frey, Bruno S., and Lorenz Goette. 1998. "Does the Popular Vote Destroy Civil Rights?" *American Journal of Political Science* 42, no. 4: 1343–8.

Gamble, Barbara S. 1997. "Putting Civil Rights to a Popular Vote." *American Journal of Political Science* 41, no. 1: 245–69.

Gerber, Elisabeth R. 1996. "Legislative Response to the Threat of Popular Initiatives." *American Journal of Political Science* 40, no. 1: 99–128.

Gerber, Elisabeth R. 1999. *The Populist Paradox: Interest Group Influence and the Promise of Direct Legislation.* Princeton, NJ: Princeton University Press.

Gerber, Elisabeth R., and Simon Hug. 2001. "Legislative Responses to Referendum." In *Referendum Democracy: Citizens, Elites, and Deliberation in Referendum Campaigns*, edited by M. Mendelsohn and A. Parkin. Toronto: Macmillan/St Martin's Press.

Gillette, Clayton P. 1988. "Plebiscites, Participation, and Collective Action in Local Government Law." *Michigan Law Review* 86, no. 5: 930–88.

Gray, Virginia. 1973. "Innovation in the States: A Diffusion Study." *American Political Science Review* 67, no. 4: 1174–85.

Grodin, Joseph R. 1988. "Developing a Consensus of Restraint: A Judge's Perspective on Judicial Retention Elections." *Southern California Law Review* 61: 1961.

Haider-Markel, Donald P. 1998. "The Politics of Social Regulatory Policy: State and Federal Hate Crime Policy and Implementation Effort." *Political Research Quarterly* 51, no. 1: 69–88.

Haider-Markel, Donald P. 2000. "Lesbian and Gay Politics in the States: Interest Groups, Electoral Politics, and Public Policy." In *The Politics of Gay Rights*, edited by Kenneth D. Wald, Craig A. Rimmerman, and Clyde Wilcox. Chicago, IL: University of Chicago Press.

Haider-Markel, Donald P. 2001. "Policy Diffusion as a Geographic Expansion of the Scope of Political Conflict: Same-Sex Marriage Bans in the 1990s." *State Politics and Policy Quarterly* 1, no. 1: 2–26.

Haider-Markel, Donald P., and Kenneth J. Meier. 1996. "The Politics of Gay and Lesbian Rights: Expanding the Scope of the Conflict." *Journal of Politics* 58, no. 2: 332–49.

Haider-Markel, Donald P., Alana Querze, and Kara Lindaman. 2007. "Lose, Win, or Draw? A Reexamination of Direct Democracy and Minority Rights." *Political Research Quarterly* 60, no. 2: 304–14.

Hajnal, Zoltan L., Elisabeth R. Gerber, and Hugh Louch. 2002. "Minorities and Direct Legislation: Evidence from California Ballot Proposition Elections." *Journal of Politics* 64, no. 1: 154–77.

Hamilton, Alexander, James Madison, and John Jay. [1787] 1999. *The Federalist Papers*, edited by Clinton Rossiter. New York: Penguin Books.

Haskell, John. 2001. *Direct Democracy or Representative Government?: Dispelling the Populist Myth*, Transforming American Politics. Boulder, CO: Westview Press.

Hate Crime Statistics Act. 1990. Public Law No.101–275. April 23, 1990.

Herek, Gregory M., and John P. Capitanio. 1995. "Black Heterosexuals' Attitudes toward Lesbians and Gay Men in the United States." *Journal of Sex Research* 32, no. 2: 95–105.

Hero, Rodney E. 1998. *Faces of Inequality: Social Diversity in American Politics.* New York: Oxford University Press.

Hero, Rodney E., and Caroline J. Tolbert. 1996. "A Racial/Ethnic Diversity Interpretation of Politics and Policy in the States of the U.S." *American Journal of Political Science* 40, no. 3: 851–71.

Jenness, Valerie, and Ryken Grattet. 2001. *Making Hate a Crime: From Social Movement to Law Enforcement.* New York: Russell Sage Foundation.

Key, V. O. 1949. *Southern Politics in State and Nation,* New York: Vintage Books.

Kittilson, Miki Caul, and Katherine Tate. 2005. "Political Parties, Minorities, and Elected Office." In *The Politics of Democratic Inclusion,* edited by Rodney E. Hero and Christina Wolbrecht. Philadelphia, PA: Temple University Press.

Kloss, Heinz. 1977. *The American Bilingual Tradition.* Rowley, MA: Newbury House.

Kranz, Rachel, and Tim Cusick. 2005. *Gay Rights.* Rev. ed., Library in a Book. New York, NY: Facts on File.

Lax, Jeffrey R., and Justin H. Phillips. 2009. "Gay Rights in the States: Public Opinion and Policy Responsiveness." *American Political Science Review* 103, no. 3: 367–86.

Lax, Jeffrey R., and Justin H. Phillips. 2009. "How Should We Estimate Public Opinion in the States?" *American Journal of Political Science* 53, no. 1: 107–21.

Lewin, Tamar. 2006. "Michigan Rejects Affirmative Action, and Backers Sue." *New York Times,* November 9, 2006.

Lewis, Daniel C. 2011. "Bypassing the Representational Filter? Minority Rights Policies under Direct Democracy Institutions in the U.S. States." *State Politics and Policy Quarterly* 11, no. 2: 198–222.

Lewis, Daniel C. 2011. "Direct Democracy and Minority Rights: Same-Sex Marriage Bans in the U.S. States." *Social Science Quarterly* 92, no. 2: 364–83.

Lewis, Daniel C., and Frederick S. Wood. 2009. "Direct Democracy, Minority Rights, and Judicial Review." Paper presented at the Annual Meeting of the Midwest Political Science Association, Chicago, IL, April 2–5.

Lupia, Arthur, Yanna Krupnikov, Adam Seth Levine, Spencer Piston, and Alexander Von Hagen-Jamar. 2010. "Why State Constitutions Differ in Their Treatment of Same-Sex Marriage." *Journal of Politics* 72, no. 4: 1222–35.

Lutz, James M. 1986. "The Spatial and Temporal Diffusion of Selected Licensing Laws in the United States." *Political Geography Quarterly* 5: 141–59.

McClosky, Herbert, and Alida Brill. 1983. *Dimensions of Tolerance: What Americans Believe About Civil Liberties.* New York: Russell Sage Foundation.

Madison, James. [1787] 1999. "No. 10: The Same Subject Continued." In *The Federalist Papers,* edited by Alexander Hamilton, James Madison, and John Jay. New York: Penguin Books.

Madison, James. [1787] 1999. "No. 51: The Structure of Government Must Furnish the Proper Checks and Balances between the Different Departments." In *The Federalist Papers,* edited by Alexander Hamilton, James Madison, and John Jay. New York: Penguin Books.

Magleby, David B. 1984. *Direct Legislation: Voting on Ballot Propositions in the United States.* Baltimore, MD: Johns Hopkins University Press.

Manweller, Mathew. 2005. "The Angriest Crocodile: Information Costs, Direct Democracy Activists, and the Politicization of State Judicial Elections." *State and Local Government Review* 37, no. 2: 86–102.

March, William. 1999. "Bush Readies Affirmative-Action Policies under Mounting Pressure." *Tampa Tribune*, November 7, 1999, 1.

Matsusaka, John G. 1995. "Fiscal Effects of the Voter Initiative: Evidence from the Last 30 Years." *Journal of Political Economy* 103, no. 3: 587–623.

Matsusaka, John G. 2004. *For the Many or the Few: The Initiative, Public Policy, and American Democracy*, American Politics and Political Economy. Chicago, IL: University of Chicago Press.

Matsusaka, John G., and Nolan M. McCarty. 2001. "Political Resource Allocation: Benefits and Costs of Voter Initiatives." *Journal of Law Economics and Organization* 17, no. 2: 413–48.

Meier, Kenneth J. 1975. "Representative Bureaucracy: An Empirical Analysis." *American Political Science Review* 69, no. 2: 526–42.

Meier, Kenneth J. 1993. "Latinos and Representative Bureaucracy Testing the Thompson and Henderson Hypotheses." *Journal of Public Administration Research and Theory: J-PART* 3, no. 4: 393–414.

Miller, Kenneth P. 2009. *Direct Democracy and the Courts*. New York: Cambridge University Press.

Mooney, Christopher Z. 2001. "State Politics and Policy Quarterly and the Study of State Politics: The Editor's Introduction." *State Politics and Policy Quarterly* 1, no. 1: 1–4.

Nicholson-Crotty, Sean. 2006. "Reassessing Madison's Diversity Hypothesis: The Case of Same-Sex Marriage." *Journal of Politics* 68, no. 4: 922–30.

Pampel, Fred C. 2004. *Racial Profiling*, Library in a Book. New York: Facts on File.

Pinello, Daniel R. 2006. *America's Struggle for Same-Sex Marriage*. New York: Cambridge University Press.

Pippen, John, Shaun Bowler, and Todd Donovan. 2002. "Election Reform and Direct Democracy: Campaign Finance Regulations in the American States." *American Politics Research* 30, no. 6: 559–82.

Preuhs, Robert R. 2005. "Descriptive Representation, Legislative Leadership, and Direct Democracy: Latino Influence on English Only Laws in the States, 1984–2002." *State Politics and Policy Quarterly* 5, no. 3: 203–24.

Qvortrup, Mads. 2001. "The Courts vs. the People: An Essay on Judicial Review of Initiatives." In *The Battle over Citizen Law Making*, edited by M. Dane Waters. Durham, NC: Carolina Academic Press.

Ranney, Austin. 1976. "Parties in State Politics." In *Politics in the American States: A Comparative Analysis*, edited by Herbert Jacob and Kenneth Nelson Vines, pp. xvii, 509. Boston, MA: Little, Brown.

Richmond, Kelly. 1996. "Assembly Bill Would End Affirmative Action by State." *The Record*, November 27, 1996, A7.

Romer, Thomas, and Howard Rosenthal. 1979. "The Elusive Median Voter." *Journal of Public Economics* 12, no. 2: 143–70.

Schattschneider, E. E. 1960. *The Semisovereign People; a Realist's View of Democracy in America*. 1st ed. New York: Holt.

Schildkraut, Deborah, J. 2001. "Official-English and the States: Influences on Declaring English the Official Language in the United States." *Political Research Quarterly* 54, no. 2: 445–57.

Schmid, Carol L. 2001. *The Politics of Language: Conflict, Identity and Cultural Pluralism in a Comparative Perspective.* New York: Oxford University Press.

Schmidt, David D. 1989. *Citizen Lawmakers: The Ballot Initiative Revolution.* Philadelphia: Temple University Press.

Schmidt, Ronald. 2000. *Language Policy and Identity Politics in the United States,* Mapping Racisms. Philadelphia, PA: Temple University Press.

Schrag, Peter. 1998. *Paradise Lost: California's Experience, America's Future.* New York: New Press; Distributed by W.W. Norton.

Slade, Stephanie, and Daniel A. Smith. 2011. "Obama to Blame? Minority Surge Voters and the Ban on Same-Sex Marriage in Florida." *The Forum* 9, no. 2.

Smith, Daniel A., and Dustin Fridkin. 2008. "Delegating Direct Democracy: Interparty Legislative Competition and the Adoption of the Initiative in the American States." *American Political Science Review* 102, no. 3: 333–50.

Smith, Daniel A., and Caroline J. Tolbert. 2004. *Educated by Initiative: The Effects of Direct Democracy on Citizens and Political Organizations in the American States.* Ann Arbor, MI: University of Michigan Press.

Smith, David M., and Gary J. Gates. 2001. "Gay and Lesbian Families in the United States: Same-Sex Unmarried Partner Households." Washington, DC: Human Rights Campaign.

Squire, Peverill. 1992. "Legislative Professionalization and Membership Diversity in State Legislatures." *Legislative Studies Quarterly* 17, no. 1: 69–79.

Squire, Peverill. 2000. "Uncontested Seats in State Legislative Elections." *Legislative Studies Quarterly* 25, no. 1: 131–46.

Squire, Peverill, and Keith E. Hamm. 2005. *101 Chambers: Congress, State Legislatures, and the Future of Legislative Studies.* Columbus, OH: Ohio State University Press.

Sullivan, J. W. 1893. *Direct Legislation by the Citizenship through the Initiative and Referendum.* New York: True Nationalist Publishing.

Tatalovich, Raymond. 1995. *Nativism Reborn?: The Official English Language Movement and the American States.* Lexington, KY: University Press of Kentucky.

Taylor, Jami K., Daniel C. Lewis, Matthew L. Jacobsmeier, and Brian DiSarro. "Content and Complexity in Policy Reinvention and Diffusion." *State Politics and Policy Quarterly* 12, no. 1: 75–98.

Tolbert, Caroline J., and John A. Grummel. 2003. "Revisiting the Racial Threat Hypothesis: White Voter Support for California's Proposition 209." *State Politics and Policy Quarterly* 3, no. 2: 183.

Tolbert, Caroline J., John Grummel, and Daniel Smith. 2001. "The Effects of Ballot Initiatives on Voter Turnout in the United States." *American Politics Research* 29, no. 6: 625–48.

Tolbert, Caroline J., and Rodney E. Hero. 1996. "Race/Ethnicity and Direct Democracy: An Analysis of California's Illegal Immigration Initiative." *Journal of Politics* 58, no. 3: 806–18.

U.S. Bureau of Justice Statistics. 1994. "Hate Crimes Reported in NIBRS, 1990–1992." edited by U.S. Department of Justice.

U.S. Bureau of Justice Statistics. 2001. "Hate Crimes Reported in NIBRS, 1997–1999." U.S. Department of Justice.

Wald, Kenneth D., James W. Button, and Barbara A. Rienzo. 1996. "The Politics of Gay Rights in American Communities: Explaining Antidiscrimination Ordinances and Policies." *American Journal of Political Science* 40, no. 4: 1152–78.

Walker, Jack L. 1969. "The Diffusion of Innovations among the American States." *American Political Science Review* 63, no. 3: 880–99.

Weber, Ronald E., and Paul Brace, eds. 1999. *American State and Local Politics: Directions for the 21st Century.* New York: Chatham House.

Wilcox, Clyde, and Robin Wolpert. 2000. "Gay Rights in the Public Sphere: Public Opinion on Gay and Lesbian Equality." In *The Politics of Gay Rights*, edited by Wald Rimmerman and Clyde Wilcox. Chicago, IL: University of Chicago Press.

INDEX